The Protected Class

The Protected Class

❖

REAL LIFE STORIES OF WOMEN OVER THE AGE OF 40 WHO HAVE EXPERIENCED DISCRIMINATION OR HARASSMENT IN THE WORKPLACE

LEGAL ACTIONS—RECOURSE RECOMMENDATIONS

Kathleen M. Hargiss, PhD MBA

Writers Club Press

San Jose New York Lincoln Shanghai

The Protected Class
REAL LIFE STORIES OF WOMEN OVER THE AGE OF 40 WHO HAVE EXPERIENCED DISCRIMINATION OR HARASSMENT IN THE WORKPLACE

Writers Club Press
an imprint of iUniverse, Inc.

For information address:
iUniverse, Inc.
5220 S. 16th St., Suite 200
Lincoln, NE 68512
www.iuniverse.com

Discrimination or harrassment could happen to you...then what are your rights? Do you just put up with it or do you do something about it?

ISBN: 0-595-24377-0

Printed in the United States of America

Contents

AFFADAVIT

Gisela Busco, Attorney at Law
Tamp, Florida

Dear Kathleen M. Hargiss:

Thank-you for giving me the opportunity to review your book titled "The Protected Class."

After carefully examining each and every one of its chapters, I was deeply impressed by its professional, instructive, and humanistic content.

Personally, I think that it serves a double purpose. On the one hand, it's useful to all those women who, in some way, can identify themselves in any of its 20 chapters, to show them that they are not alone., that several ways or paths exist which can be followed or doors which can be knocked on in order to make their rights be heard.

On the other hand, the book shows the legal profession the need which exists in obtaining a unified regulation which specifically takes these cases into account.

Once again please receive my sincere congratulations. I believe that this is a book that will be read often in search of advice and guidance for situations which come up daily in our jobs.

Sincerely,

Gisela Busco
Attorney at Law

Special Thanks to Attorney Gisela Busco for the long hours dedicated to reviewing the legal areas of the book. Counselor, your input was invaluable.

PREFACE

Intent of the book: To share professional work experiences of women over the age of forty. The stories involve the frustrations that women have experienced in the work place due to their age, gender, or attained educational level. By sharing these experiences, others may learn what their legal rights are in work-related situations.

Some of the interviews appeared bittersweet, some serious, and a few were quite humorous. In addition, several interviews were quite lengthy while others were short and concise. Please note, not every situation needed the expertise of trained legal professionals. Although all the interviews shared one commonality, and that was the interviews were all based on real life experiences.

The underlying element that prevailed throughout many of the interviews was the 'fear factor'. Women admitted they were afraid to pursue legal action(s). One of the major reasons was based on the accumulation of a huge legal bill that would take years to pay off. Another factor evident in almost all the interviews was the fear of sharing too much personal information. There seemed to be an omnipresent apprehension that someone would find out what they were revealing and use it against them at a future date. Even though they admitted they were telling the truth, the fear of possible consequences was a reality difficult to face. Most women openly admitted they wanted justice, but were not prepared or ready to pay an extreme price.

Years ago it was unusual to see a specific chapter in a business law text dedicated to employment rights. Situations that occurred on the job would have been normally handled by a designated person in charge of company policies, the human resource department, or both.

Today individuals are privy to the fact that they have a right to contact a governmental agency for assistance in work related matters.

Agencies such as the Equal Employment Opportunity Commission (EEOC) and the Age Discrimination in Employment (ADEA) are available to help employees in need. Legal information concerning these agencies is placed at the end of certain interviews where the rules applied. This information should be simply referred to as reference material in which a reader may use as a guide in order to pursue legal action, if needed. Please note, this book is not meant as a substitute for qualified legal advice. Information will be provided and may be used at the reader's discretion. It is up to the reader to decide what type of action(s), if any, is needed to pursue in remedying a particular situation(s). Also, be aware that not all the stories in the book have laws to protect the individuals. In some cases, there is no recourse and no appropriate or available legal remedy or remedies.

Format: The structural plans for the text were to be based on a series of middle and line management experiences. The first part of each chapter is called the "descriptive analysis" which offers either a definition, explanation of the problem, or a combination of both. The second section is titled the "interview" which includes an interview based on a true-life experience. The third part is twofold; a description of the "action" the interviewee pursued after the incident or incidents were over, followed by a "recourse" section that includes possible legal solution(s). This section will vary in format structure from interview to interview. Some endings appear to have an empathetic effect, some for legal prescription, and some illustrate life lessons.

The research format consisted of a qualified interviewee and an interviewer. In order to qualify for this research study an interviewee had to meet the following criteria: (1) female, (2) over the age of forty, and (3) experienced an unfortunate situation or situations in the work place. The average interview lasted about two hours. In order to protect the interviewees, fictional names were substituted for real names and a private consent form signed. This consent form promised total protection/privacy of individual identities.

The approach used was due to the volunteers in this study who expressed fear that the information would possibly uncover their identity and affect hiring decisions of future employers. Many felt they would be forced to relocate in a different part of the country in order to obtain employment.

Legal terms: The words used in law very often appear similar to a foreign language. The frustrating part is that the words themselves rarely mean what they seem. Quite a few of the legal terms/words seem to have everyday English meanings, but unfortunately have very different technical definitions.

Whenever a legal word or term is used in this book, it will appear as *italicized* in order to bring it to the reader's attention. Most of the time the term or word will be defined in the text, but for some reason it is eliminated, refer to Chapter Twenty; "Legal Definitions Defined." This chapter includes a list of definitions referring to the legal terms and words used in this book.

Necessary definitions: The following definitions are included at this time in order to enable the reader to achieve a better understanding of the contents in this book:

- **Employers** are not allowed to discriminate in employment interviews, hiring, upgrading, recruiting, discharging, and setting working conditions.

- **Employees** must not be denied employment because of race, color, religion, national origin, sex, age, marital status, and mental or physical handicap.

- **Newspapers** are not allowed to publish discriminatory employment advertisements.

- **Employment Agencies** are not allowed to discriminate in job referrals, ask pre-employment questions or pass out information that limits employment because of race, color, religion, national origin, sex, age, marital status, mental or physical handicap.

- **Labor Organizations** are not allowed to deny membership to qualified people or discriminate in apprentice training programs.

- **Landlords, Realtors, Sellers** are not allowed to discriminate based on race, color, religion, sex, national origin, marital status, mental or physical handicap in the sale, rental, leasing of real property. The law also forbids any kind of discrimination in the financing of real property.

Qualifications of the Interviewer/Author: Kathleen M. Hargiss holds a Ph.D., M.B.A, M.A, B.S. and European Post Graduate study degrees. Dr. Hargiss has instructed and conducted research at the following institutions: Northwestern University, University of Chicago, University of South Florida, and the University of Tampa. In the last twenty-five years, Dr. Hargiss has accumulated experiences in a variety of business related areas. She is currently completing three books, and serves as a consultant for a Tampa-based firm.

Disclaimer: The reader should understand that the information provided in this book is not rendered by legal or professional services. The contents of this book were written by a researcher and not by a lawyer. The information in this text is provided to assist individuals that are confronted with discrimination or harassment. The text includes information intended to help individuals learn their rights, gain access to applicable laws, find ways for resolution, and locate competent counsel. The author and the publisher disclaim any liability, loss or risk incurred as a consequence(s), either directly or indirectly, of the application and use of the informational contents here within. This information should not be used as a substitute for the advice of legal counsel or other law professionals.

INTRODUCTION

The Bureau of Labor Statistics has reported that more women are working than ever before. In the last century the number of working women have grown from 5.3 million in 1900 to 18.4 million in 1950 and to 63 million in 1997.

The Department of Labor in 1987 published a report titled "Workforce 2000. This report brought attention to the changes that were taking place in the economy in relation to the composition of the workforce. Certain data associated with minorities and women proved to be increasing in importance. Since the publication of this document, the evidence collaborated further illustrates that minorities and women have made significant gains in entering and re-entering the workforce.

Let's start at the beginning. What is the Women's Bureau and what does it accomplish? Many women have never heard about this governmental department as witnessed in a majority of the interviews. In the past seventy-years, the Women's Bureau has been seen as a strong voice for the female minority but also as a helping hand for working women. The bureau is one of the oldest agencies in the U.S. Department of Labor. Officially, the Women's Bureau was created and instituted by Congress on June 5, 1920. The official mandate stated: "standards formulated with policies that shall promote the welfare of 'wage-earning-women'. The original concepts were to improve working conditions, increase efficiency, and advance profitable employment opportunities. These actions were predicated upon the long working hours of women in unsafe and unhealthy environments, while earning below standard wages. Due to these oppressive conditions, Congress was urged to establish a Federal agency that would investigate and document work-life oppression experienced by women along with recommended changes. In 1938, the Fair Labor Standards Act was passed establishing the first Federal hour and wage law.

Well into World War II (1940's) the Bureau assisted the nation in meeting industrial requirements while the men were serving in the military. The Bureau encouraged women to enter the industry by providing training programs. Keeping in mind that these women had child care needs, the bureau provided centers for adequate care.

In the 1950's and the 1960's, the Bureau realized the need to address specific issues ranging from education to career oriented training, which successfully resulted in the Equal Pay Act. The Bureau also proved instrumental in the promotion of the President's Commission on the Status of Women (1961).

The 1970's revealed an abundance of women joining the workforce. The Bureau heavily promoted women's employment training along with career choice positioning. Important aspects of the Bureau were seen in the promotion of women into non-traditional trade jobs, professional specialties, and the inclusion into upper corporate management level positions. These opportunities generally paid higher wages, offered mobility and fringe benefits.

In the 1980's, the phenomena of the dual breadwinner household grew. More families were supported by single adults, and mothers with preschool children entering the labor force in droves. The main issues that erupted were in the area of familial care needs. This proved to be pertinent due to the working mother's need in allocating time to her job and children. It is interesting that during this time women made quantum leaps in the areas of education and all occupations. Women were making a significant stand!

The 1990's rolled in and special attention by the Women's Bureau was focused on policy development and procedures that would enable the balancing of family and work responsibilities. The Women's Bureau is already recognized as favorably responding to the times by instituting the Work and Family Clearinghouse. This is a computerized data base that suggests options for helping female workers resolve conflicts in relation to balancing their family and work responsibilities.

Seen in the late 1990's and presently in the year 2000, women having raised their families are re-entering the workforce. Most of these women are over the age of forty and are now attempting to regain the foothold they once previously held before resigning in order to undertake the responsibilities of motherhood. These women are now experiencing problems not only in regaining their once held positions, but also in attempting in to re-enter the workforce. Problems are arising between employers and employees leading to discriminatory actions.

Women have always encountered barriers to employment advancement. Today is better, but not that much different from the time females first entered the workplace environment. The following survey results illustrate today's existing problems.

Women: "Top Five Barriers To Advancement" (10-17-2000)

*Note: On a scale from 1 to 5...one represents no barrier at all...five represents a significant barrier

- Corporate culture favors men   4.01

- Stereotyping/preconceptions of women   3.85

- Lack of women on board   3.69

- Exclusion from informal networks   3.55

- Perception by management that family respon- 3.54
  sibilities will interfere

Everyone needs to remember the principle that all men and women are created equal. In addition, that applies to the employer's treatment of employees in the workplace.

This book is about a search for life's meaning as well as financial gains. Women expressed the need for a meaningful life rather than a mere existence of Monday through Friday, nine to five toil. The females interviewed all expressed the desire to be treated fairly in the field of employment, and be given an equal chance along with every-one else.

As a reminder, some of the interviews are bittersweet to where the reader's heart will go out to the victim. Whereas, other interviews show strength and the willingness to fight for a cause. Some readers will find themselves associating with one or more of the interviewees and their experience(s). Hopefully, the content of this book may increase the readers awareness as to the reality of workplace injustice(s) and what can be done about it.

*The Wall Street Journal (10-17-2000). Cultural Conflict: Women and Minorities Continue to Take a Back Seat in Business. New York, Recruitment Diversity Career Journal.

1

THE GLASS CEILING

The glass ceiling has been described as the artificial barriers that deny minorities and women from advancing in their careers. Thousands of qualified women and minoritiy members each year are denied access to top level jobs in corporate America. Reports state that the glass ceiling barriers exist at all levels of organizations and at different levels in industries. Even though CEO's have an increasinging awareness of managerial diversity in the workplace, women and minoirities are still being denied the opportunity to hold senior level positions in the private sector.

Disparities still exist for women and minorities, for example; equal educational attained levels are not a guarantee for fair financial compensation. Reports show that women have a considerable lower mean incomes than their male counterparts. Interesting, women that hold bachelor, master, and post graduate degrees is steadily increasing. And in addition it is important to point out that the areas of discipline are not restricted to teaching, nursing, etc., but are also in law and business. Despite having the educational credentials that qualify women for senior management positions along with career commitment…men are still progressing at a faster rate than women.

In 1991, Title II of the Civil Rights Act established the "Federal Glass Ceiling Commission." It was classified as a twenty-one member bipartisan commission appointed by President George Bush. The purpose of the commission was to study and recommend ways to eliminate the barriers women and minorities experience when attempting to advance into management and decision-making positions in the private sector. The actionable goal was to present an annual Presidential award to a business who has made significant efforts to remove obstacles to career growth and has provided advancement opportunities to minorities and women. This also included the education of the general public on who is effectively by and what can be done to remove glass ceiling barriers. Note:

The commission first task was to identify the barriers that prevent minorities and women from advancing in the workplace.:

1. Governmental barriers include unclear data in reference to various groups at the managerial level. Laws already enacted need to be enforced.

2. Societal barriers incluidie the number of educational opportunities afforded and the job attainment level.

3. Sterotypical thinking, either manifested through the conscious or the unconscious will produce a certain bias. Simply stated: many employers hire individuals who look like them or fit the company's image. Many times these stereotypes, if conveniently ignored, develop into factual popular beliefs that reinfoce the barriers associated with the glass ceiling.

The Glass Ceiling Commission unanimously agreed upon several ways to shatter the barriers that prevent women and minorities from achieving upper management level positions. According to Labor Secretary Robert B. Reich, the previous chairperson of the Commission: "Equity demands that we destroy the glass ceiling. Smart business demands it as well." (U.S. Dept. of Labor Office of Public Affairs Washington, D.C, 1995).

The Commission completed its legislarive mandate in 1999 under the leadership of the Secretary of Labor, Robert Reich. Interesting to note; the Commission accepted all recommendations on its last day of work. Immediately following, the Commission was terminated by law.

The published report titled; "A Solid Investment:: Making Full Use of the Nation's Human Capital (U.S. Department of Labor Office of Public Affairs Washington D.C.) presented to President Clinton and select committees of the Congress illustrates finings and recommendations that in dissolving the glass ceiling concept will help the American workforce transit into the middle class and beyond. The report addressed ways in which government, business, and society as a whole can help destroy the glass ceiling concept.

The following is an overview of the Commission's suggestions to shatter the concept of the Glass Ceiling:

1. Americ'a businesses need to fully utilize the nation's capital, this would result in solid investments.

2. Bias and discrimination must be banished from the executive boardrooms in order for real change to occur.

3. Efforts to achieve diversity in the workplace should be included in the corporate strategic business plans.

4. Corporations should demonstrate and promote CEO commitment

5. Utilize affirmative action as a tool

6. Employee education as to ethnic, racial and gender diversity

7. Promote family friendly policies

8. Government needs to lead by example

9. Increase enforcement of existing antidiscrimination laws

The above suggestions look good in print. But realistically speaking, the government must take an active role in shattering the glass ceiling. It must enforce the concepts of equal access and opportunity and not rely on the private sector to complete all the work. Enforcement agencies must become aggressive in enforcing antidiscrimination laws and update policies and regulations in order to keep in pace with the ever changing work environment. And in addition, these government agencies be must supplied with adequate fincanial resources in order to enforce legislative mandates.

The glass ceiling carries with it the attitudes of society at large. The government recognizes the difficulty in altering human attitudes and realizes these changes cannot be mandated, dictated or even legislated. The commission has promoted initiatives to address a variety of barriers in hopes of reducing stereotypical thinking which carries along with it prejudice and bias.

Cracks are seen in the glass ceiling and women and minorities are moving up corporate ladders but still at a very slow pace. Corporate America must realize the importance of the inclusion of these groups. The business world has to acknowledge the need for talent at the highest levels to better compete with changing consumer markets, demographics and international competition in the present economy.

Research has not embraced the perception that "many white males as a group are losing—losing competitive advantage, losing control, and losing opportunity as a direct consequence of inclusion of women and minorities." (R. Redwood, The Glass Ceiling)

The real-life stories you are about to read all encompass the difficulties many have experienced in the workplace. At the end of the book, take a moment to reflect and ask yourself; " Has the glass ceiling really shattered or is it a reality we must continue to bear?"

2

AGE DISCRIMINATION
"Catherine's story"

Descriptive Analysis: The work force in America is aging with baby boomers remaining in their careers longer than in the past. These individuals generally move up the corporate ladder, thus acquiring more benefits and higher salaries. Resultantly, employers face the dilemma of maintaining a more mature-senior group.

A problem that usually arises for this age group includes increasing layoffs, generally referred to by most companies as "right sizing." This group then encounters difficulties finding new forms of employment in the midst of an economic boom.

There is another segment of these baby boomers that due to circumstances have to return to the workplace at a later time in life. It is difficult for many people over the age of forty to find employers that will hire an older individual. If you are an individual born with terrific genes and appear ageless, then more opportunities will be available.

Problems sometimes occur when the individual's true age is revealed. Age should not be a concern, for it should be predicated on the individual's job performance. However, this is America where many of the standards are skewed, placing a greater emphasis upon a youthful appearance. The government has realized this mindset and has established certain protectorates for the older worker.

The *Age Discrimination in Employment Act (ADEA)* protects an individual from being discriminated against because of age, but only if the individual is over forty and is employed by an organization with at least twenty people. Although it depends on the state, the individual resides. Note: there are human rights laws that protect the individual even if they are under the age of forty.

Qualifications for an *Age Discrimination Case*:

- Individual is in a protected age group (over 40)

- Individuals' termination was justified as circumstances that are referenced to age. (In other words, the individual was passed over for a promotion by a younger employee)

- Individual was dismissed, demoted or the main issue of an adverse job decision

- Individual was qualified for the position.

All rules have exceptions and the ADEA is not atypical:

- If your age is an occupational qualification for the job, then an individual can be terminated when that age becomes an important fact. This rule has been upheld many times, for example: fire fighters and police personal.

- If you have held an executive position for the past two years, entitled to an immediate (non-forfeitable pension) of at least $44,000 per year, then you may be required to step-down at the age of 65.

- If you are terminated because of a: retirement plan, apprentice system or a seniority system.

Now is the time to read Catherine's story. See if you think she was justified filing age discrimination charges?

Interview: Meet Catherine, a lovely, tall, blonde haired woman in her early fifties. Catherine related her story with a certain elegance and ease, even though it proved to be difficult at times.

She immediately expressed a desire to start the interview by presenting a picture of how her life was before the nightmare took place. Catherine turned and looked out the window, quietly reminiscing of a time in her life that had a special place in her heart.

After taking a deep breath she started the interview by saying, she wanted the reader to picture a couple attending their twin girl's college graduation. Finally reaching the point in life where Catherine and her husband Bob could make plans for just the two of them. About one month after attending the graduation, Catherine's husband Bob became ill. Thinking he had a touch of the flu, Bob just shrugged it off. Until they both noticed how much weight he was losing. That was about the middle of May.

The first thing that came to Catherine's mind was to suggest that Bob should make an appointment with the family general practitioner, so through her persistence, he finally did. After completing a few exams, the doctor insisted that Bob see an oncologist. It was in the oncologist's office that Catherine's world came to a halt.

Unfortunately, the tests came back with horrific news. Bob had been diagnosed with colon cancer. The tumor could be removed from the colon, but the seriousness lay in the area of the liver. The files showed that over sixty-percent of the organ was infected. Surgery was immediately planned to remove the tumor. Their family doctor tried to manage their expectations by explaining that the experts do not know how much of an organ has been damaged, until they actually open the person up.

Sitting in the hospital waiting room, Catherine knew as soon as she saw the surgeon that it was not good news. As she sat for eight hours waiting for Bob to come out of the recovery room, she watched other surgeons come out of the hallway and meet with the waiting families. Usually these surgeons had big smiles on their faces and hugs for the waiting family. When Bob's surgeon appeared he waved to her to come in to the inner hallway. A few tears streaked down Catherine's cheek as she recalled the day. She said a chill went down her spine, for she knew immediately and was not surprised at the surgeon's news.

It seems that the cancer had spread to over eighty percent of the liver, and it would only be a matter of a week or two. Catherine went on to explain that she felt herself floating, almost like being in a dream like state. As she brushed a tear from her cheek, she continued to say that she remembered walking silently out of the hospital and sitting on a bench. The tears silently running down her cheeks eventually turned into sobs. Not realizing anyone was there, all of a sudden she felt a warm hand on her shoulder. As she turned to see who it was, she felt a peacefulness come across her. The person standing next to was an elderly man with the biggest blue eyes she had ever seen. The strangest thing about the encounter was that neither one spoke, but just sat in silence. This complete stranger coming out of nowhere evidently was there to comfort her. In her mind raced a mirage of thoughts. What was she to do? Bob and the girls had been her whole life for as long as she could remember. Now what?

Regaining her strength she thanked the old man and then immediately found a telephone and called the twins. In a very matter of fact manner, she told the girls what the situation was and asked them to come home immediately. After the call, she walked back into the hospital and sat patiently waiting for Bob to come out of surgery.

Two hours passed, and down the hallway, Catherine could see the nurses wheeling Bob towards his hospital room. As she approached the room, she prayed that she could have the strength to tell him what the diagnosis was. Bob and Catherine made a promise earlier, no matter how bad the news was they would be honest with each other.

Walking into Bob's room, she seemed taken back by his demeanor. Bob weakly smiled, took her hand and nodded that he already knew. "Be strong my darling, for I need you now more than I ever have in our entire marriage."

The girls arrived late that night. Thank heavens for Hospice, for they prepared Catherine as how to handle the twins and how to manage her own emotions. For what was to come was a fast speeding train loaded with a car load of nightmares, the kind most people pray they will never have to experience. One week later, Bob died.

Still in shock, Catherine sat and pondered what to do with the rest of her life. For the only life she knew came to a crashing halt when Bob left. She had not given it another thought, for life was just beginning for them.

Catherine was in the retail business before she met Bob. She held a prestigious position with one of the top firms in the city, but that was twenty years ago…now what? Getting her resume' together and sending out a few thousand copies seemed to be and endless job in itself, but she knew it had to be done.

A few months passed without a bite from anyone in the business. Sitting and having coffee with an old friend, she finally got her first lead. Her friend knew of an acquaintance that owned a retail business. She said she would give him a call, but did not know if there was a position open. Two days later the friend contacted Catherine and told her to call this number immediately for a position had opened up just that very morning.

Catherine did not care what the requirements of the job were, for she was at a point of despair. At times, she found herself second-guessing her ability to get back into the work force. That afternoon she found herself sitting in the office of Human Resources being interviewed by a heavy-set, balding man in his late forties. He was impressed as to her qualifications but did not have a job to match. What he did have was a sales position and wanted to know if she was interested. He recommended taking this position in order to get her foot back in the door. Maybe in due time a position that could utilize her abilities would open. The HR representative reminded her that being in the right place at the right time was more important than having a degree from a top ten university in the country. Therefore, Catherine accepted the job.

It was a medium-sized company with a staff of around thirty. Being tight on space, Catherine shared an office with the retail store manager. The company had two divisions, one relating to mail order and the other an onsite store. The woman she shared the office with was responsible for managing the store on a daily basis.

As time went on, Catherine realized why this woman was not pleased with the office arrangement. The manager was running two businesses, one for the company and one for herself. Her business involved taking kickbacks and selling lines of merchandise, sometimes in direct competition with her employer. Catherine tried to mind her own business and usually looked the other way or excused herself from the office when the manager was reeling and dealing. Inside Catherine kept asking herself why she wasn't managing the store. To even the casual observer it was obvious that the store needed an over-hauling, all the things Catherine had been prepared for and was qualified to do.

About four months into the job, Catherine was summoned to the General Manager's office. This was a total surprise since she only had the opportunity of having two meetings with this man. The General Manager was on the telephone when she entered the office. He immediately looked up from his desk and motioned her to be seated. Quietly she took a seat in a big oversized leather chair sitting directly in front of his desk. Glancing around the office she noticed that he had a degree from the University of Ohio and had only graduated ten years previous. Trying not to stare, she did glance at him and noticed that he was a nice looking man in his early thirties. Wondering how much experience, he had for his young years and how he had landed this position.

After concluding his telephone call, he turned toward Catherine and stated matter of fatly that he was pleased with her work and that he critically reviewed her resume' in which he was dually impressed. Why he asked her into his office was quite clear, he had made the decision to eliminate the store manager's position and was wondering if she would be interested. Catherine almost fell on the floor in amazement. According to what happened next is that she found herself stuttering in an attempt to say "yes, I would be honored."

The General Manager smiled with approval and continued into a conversation as what he wanted to be done with the store, especially financially. Catherine reassured him that there should not be a problem, but would take a little time in redesigning and reworking specific areas. Looking pleased he continued on expressing his delight in Catherine's decision.

The only thing that disturbed Catherine was the way the company intended to eliminate the present managerial position. The General Manager suggested that he call the corporate office in Phoenix and talk to the company's counsel. After a few minutes, the General Manager started a casual but polite conversation with the corporate attorney, John Sloan. Few minutes passed when the General Manager turned towards Catherine and informed the attorney that a third party was present. After the courteous introductions, the attorney asked if there were any problems to be foreseen in the dismissal of the managerial position. The young General Manager sat in silence, so Catherine asked permission to intercede with her thoughts. "John, I don't see any adversarial recourse by this woman due to the fact that she is over the age of forty. If this position is going to be incorporated as part of my job responsibility then there should not be a problem, for I am not only female but over fifty. When the General Manager heard this, he blurted out "If I knew you were over fifty I would never had hired you." The room went silent, one could hear a pin drop. There was a deafening silence from the corporate attorney, and then realizing what a stupid comment he made, the General Manager laughed nervously.

Catherine graciously uncrossed her long legs, and almost in a balletic style rose to her feet and smoothly exited the office. As she walked from the office, she felt a sense of shock creep over her body. Here she had toiled for months in a low, paying position only to be insulted about her age. Catherine then wondered, what would happen from here on out?

Catherine continued in her position for the next three months. Hoping in that time, she could land something else. Even though Bob had left her financially secure, she knew she needed a purpose and wanted a goal. This she knew would get her up in the morning and out the door.

In the last three months, she reorganized the store, re-trained the staff, cleaned out excess inventory, re-ordered stock that she felt would move, and overall started to produce a profit. However, unfortunately the self-accounting she kept from day to day did not reflect in the comptroller's books.

One day at the beginning of the second month, she arranged a meeting with the accountant. It seems the commissions promised by the general manager did not show up on her paycheck, and she wanted to know why. According to the books, the retail store lost money. Catherine questioned the numbers, her daily tally showing the opposite. She knew that when her predecessor was operating the store, it did lose money on a regular monthly basis. But how could this be, after all the hard work and long hours she spent cleaning up the mess, she could not comprehend why she was not receiving her just compensation. The accountant informed Catherine that there must be a mistake and he would check into it and get back to her. The second month passed and stills no news from the accounting office. It happened once again. The second month should have reflected an even greater profit, but once again, the accountant reported an incredible loss. Then came the call from the accounting department. The reason Catherine was not receiving a commission was that the inventory count was still incorrect. Once again, Catherine questioned the accuracy of the statement and found it to be false.

If the inventory count was off maybe there was a mistake. She immediately returned to the store and questioned her staff as to how the inventory count was conducted. The staff unanimously agreed to re-do the inventory. At the end of eight more grueling hours counting each minute item, the inventory did not show any digressions. Just before concluding the inventory, Catherine quickly jumped to her feet and blurted out that she knew the source of the problem. Certain cosmetic items were stored in the adjacent salon that should have been included in the inventory. The inventory count was perfect for the store but no one remembered that a certain percent of the inventory was not in-house. Jeannie, a relatively new-member to the staff looked at Annie and said, "Let's go." The two of them rushed off to the salon and completed the final inventory.

After receiving the numbers, Catherine hurried to the accounting department and explained what had happened. The accountant said she was pleased with Catherine's findings and would discuss the details with the general manager.

Feeling relieved, Catherine walked out of the office thinking that things would be revised. Once again, nothing was done, and once again, she did not receive her just commission. Even though she was still performing her first job in sales, she theoretically was not being paid for the work performed in the store.

Frustration set in which gradually turned to anger. Catherine had requested a set of the financials only to find that the general manager was plugging the numbers. The General Manager had been manipulating the numbers in order to look successful in the corporate office, and in so doing, was cheating Catherine out of her compensation. After confronting the General Manager, in a very soft but direct way, she knew it would be a very short matter of time before he would find a flimsy excuse to fire her, or make it so miserable that she would voluntarily resign. And he did, she resigned voluntarily one week later.

Action: Catherine filed *age discrimination* charges with the *EEOC*. She was apprehensive about filing the charges. Her brother, an attorney with a large law firm, was the obvious person to ask for help. After describing the situation on the phone, he agreed with her and told her she had a "prima facie" case. Joe informed Catherine that the manager did not have any right saying: "If I knew you were over fifty I would never had hired you…" The second point Joe felt was important was the presence of a key witness, and that turned out to be the corporate attorney, John Sloan.

According to Joe, it was a solid case. He proved right. Six weeks after filing the charges with the *EEOC*, Catherine elected to go into mediation. After two hours, both parties agreed to a financial settlement.

At the end of the interview, Catherine expressed a sense of relief that it was all over and fortunately did not drag out for years. Catherine explained that although the case ended victorious, she still felt bad; for once again, she was out of a job. Then reconsidering everything that had transpired, it was gratifying to receive some financial remuneration for the way she was treated.

Recourse: Before rushing off and filing a charge with the *EEOC*, always stop and first examine the merits of the case. Answer the following questions and if you still feel adamant about taking action then do so...

1. Are you in the protected age group? (which is over forty years and over)

2. Where you fired, demoted, or the object of an adverse job decision?

3. Where you dismissed based upon your age?

4. Where you replaced or passed over for a promotion by a younger employee?

5. Where you qualified for the promotion but passed over?

Remember that your employer also has rights. Being over forty does not give you carte blanche to do what ever you like. The employer may win along the lines that your untimely dismissal was not due to your age or job performance, but due to unexpected circumstances experienced by the company. The company may be going through financial hardships, and their future is uncertain. The company may have to make critical decisions, either down size, make other cut backs or file for bankruptcy.

It is extremely difficult to win a discrimination case if you are fired and not replaced. Instead, your duties may be allocated to other employees in the department.

In one actual case, the president of the company fired an employee because he thought the individual's salary was too high in relation to current market conditions. Justified...the court ruled in his favor.

Here are the steps to be taken to bring an action against your employer based on age. These rules must be adhered to in order to preserve your claim.

1. The charge must be filed within 180 days of the alleged discriminatory action(s)

2. In some states, the EEOC charge requires filing within 300 days. Check to see what the EEOC's requirements are in the state in which you reside.
    To contact the EEOC: 1-800-669-3362 or 206-220-6883 (Seattle)
    http://www.eeoc.gov

3. An age claim lawsuit must be filed within 90 days after the receipt of a 'right-to-sue' letter is received from the *EEOC*.

Note: If you fail to follow the required *EEOC's* time periods you may relinquish your rights to seek a remedy for age discrimination under the rulings of the *ADEA*. Also, remember that with time passing, crucial evidence may be lost along with valuable witnesses who memories may be fading.

A serious individual filing a claim would be wise to seek professional counsel. These *employment law* experts can make sure that the proper paper work is not only completed but also presented within the required time lines

The question that most individuals spend time contemplating is: "How can I prove age *discrimination?*" First, the United States Supreme Court has specific guidelines to follow to determine whether *age discrimination* has occurred:

1. The individual must be a member of the class protected by the statute

2. The individual has suffered an adverse employment action

3. The individual was clearly qualified for the position.

4. The individual was treated unfairly compared to other company employers.

Note: Direct evidence does not have to be produced in order to prove an employer's discriminatory intent. The individual may rely on indirect proof.

Another question that should be answered initially is: "What do you want to achieve in filing *charges* against your employer?"

1. Do you want to be reinstated in your previous position?

2. Do you want to recover back wages and benefits?

3. Do you want the employer to pay the attorney's fees?

4. Do you want the employer (if the case goes to trial) pay the court costs?

Note: You may have a combination of reasons, but be sure you understand your motives completely.

Recovery:

1. *Liquidated damages* may be awarded in the same amount as lost back pay, benefits, or both.

2. If you are unable to return to your previously held position, the court may award a dollar amount for future loss of earnings and Benefits. This is usually calculated over a specifically stated number of years.

3. *Damages* may be recovered for a time up to two years.

4. *Recovery* does not include punitive damages or emotional distress.

5. Depending on the situation, you may be eligible for additional recoveries under state law, rather than federal law.

Most claims are resolved by conciliation, with the following possible outcomes:

- Damages

- Apology(s)

- Withdrawal of the charge(s)

- Job appointment

- Reinstatement

- Promotion

- Changes in practices and policies

Note: This type of action scares many people, for they are either entering into a legal area that they know very little, or nothing about. At times, you may start to second-guess yourself as to why you initiated all this to begin with. A competent attorney may offer experienced advice and guidance that may help you attain a better settlement.

It is always advantageous for an experienced attorney to review all pertinent facts of your case, and in so doing, may alleviate any fear of the unknown that you may experience.

In conclusion, remember there are many more intricacies involved with the *EEOC/ADEA* than have been examined in this book. This is a broad overview designed to familiarize you with your rights and how to take action. Hiring an attorney that is willing to work with you on a retainer basis may be the way to proceed. Remember, if you win, your attorney wins, and if you loose, your attorney looses. A sharp lawyer will only take a case he/she is assured that will be successful…and that means it is well worth your time.

NOTE: If the *EEOC* fails to resolve the complaint to the individual's satisfaction, then additional action may take place resulting in a *lawsuit*. In addition, if the individual resides in a state that prohibits *discrimination*, the individual may elect to file a complaint under either federal (*ADEA*), state law, or both

3

SLEEPING WITH THE BOSS
"Maria's Story"

Descriptive Analysis: Sleeping with the boss is a major fax-paux. It will only get the individual into trouble, maybe not right away, but eventually. This sort of behavior is not acceptable in business or any other field.

Interview: Maria made the quintessential mistake of dating her boss. During the interview she commented six times as what a "dumb thing to do." When she first interviewed for the job, Maria was going through a tough and nasty divorce. All she wanted was to get a job that would take her mind off the craziness in her life. She was also desperate for financial freedom, since her husband would not allow her the checkbook, but gave her a pittance each week to run the house.

Intending on landing a job, she did not notice how the manager was checking her out during the interview. "Honestly" Maria said, my first impression of him was good, he was nice looking and seemed to be very interested in her well being. He appeared extremely sincere and went out of his way to make her comfortable during the interview. After about an hour, Maria was offered the position, which she immediately accepted.

Two weeks into the new job, she realized more was expected of her than what was on the surface. Her boss would constantly go out of his way in order to engage her in simple conversation.

One day after a long night of fighting with her soon to be ex-husband, Maria found herself completely drained and literally exhausted. Sitting at her desk the next day, she felt like the world was ready to collapse, when her boss approached her with an invitation to have dinner. "Hey he said: "It's Friday night, tomorrow is a day of leisure, why not start out with a little fun. You know Maria; if you cooperate with me, I can make your life around the office rather nice. Maybe over a candle lit dinner, we can discuss possibilities of a promotion and time off for a little rest and relaxation." Surprised and taken off guard as to his out spoken demeanor, she found herself struggling for words. The next thing she knew, was accepting his invitation for dinner.

Maria had no idea what was to happen in the next few hours. Being upset about the divorce made her forget everything, which included eating breakfast and lunch. Going out after work for dinner seemed like a good idea. She unfortunately never thought twice about not eating anything all day.

Her boss met her in the parking lot and escorted her to his car. On the way, he asked her if she enjoyed French food for there was a charming little café down on the bayshore. During her marriage with Carlos, the only type of restaurants he would take her to where in the Spanish community. Even though she grew up eating black beans and rice, it would have been nice one in awhile to have tried different types of food and restaurants. When they pulled up in front of the restaurant, her boss immediately jumped out of the car, and came around to her side to open the car door. Never before had anyone ever given Maria that type of respect. She admitted in a sheepish manner that she rather enjoyed the special attention. Little did she know, she would be paying a high price?

The maitre de welcomed her boss by his first name. Maria noticed the money being transferred during the handshake. The maitre de' escorted Maria and her boss to a beautiful table over looking the bay. Candlelight, wine, and an exquisite dinner, Maria thought this was too good to be true. He constantly told her how beautiful she was and what a great time he was having. Maria thought to herself, here she was turning forty-one, soon to be divorced and being courted by her boss.

One drink led to the next, dinner was a blur, and time passed by fast. The next thing she knew was waking up the next morning with her boss snoring loudly next to her in bed. That was the beginning of the end.

Maria enjoyed the attention at first, but then started resenting her boss's license to do what he wanted with her. It turned into more than casual flirtations. He would take increasingly unwanted liberties, by slapping her on the butt or making lewd remarks of how wonderful she was the night they slept together. Not wanting to give up her job, Maria wondered how much longer she could put up with these unwanted advances.

About two months into the job, her boss asked her if she was interested in taking a long weekend in the Bahamas. Maria admitted, she really did not know what to do. If she did not go along with his wishes, she would probably be out of a job and back on the street peddling her resume'. Then she thought, why not, no one will know.

The trip was exciting and wonderful. She had never been to the islands and everything seemed to appear like a paradise. Her boss fell over backwards to make her feel special, something she needed after years of abuse with her now ex-husband. He was the first man to actually treat her like a queen. The only thing that bothered her was some of his fantasies in the bedroom. A few seemed rather peculiar, but after being married to a Carlos, nothing really shocked her anymore.

The six-month review was scheduled with each employe. Maria had never been through a review and was not quite sure what to expect. Twenty-minutes after the session began the senior evaluatin committee unanimously awarded Maria an outstanding performance review.. She knew she had worked hard and because of this became the top producer in the office. Even though she tried to keep her relationship with her boss a secret, she had a funny feeling her co-workers all knew.

Handling her boss up to this point did not appear to be a problem. Then the day arrived, when his wife showed up at work demanding to talk with her. This was the last thing she had expected. It was a nasty scene. The woman walked in and marched up to Maria's desk, demanding an explanation of why Maria was sleeping with her husband. The story the boss gave her from the start was that he was in the midst of a divorce. Surprise, not only married, but three kids at home to support.

Maria stated, she had an extremely difficult time continuing after the incident. "I guess my co-workers lost respect for me." A few of the guys would stand around my desk discussing their sexual activities while telling off-color jokes. They would then look at me and wink. One guy even went so far as referring to me as babe."

The workplace became extremely uncomfortable. Maria openly admitted as to the difficult time she was experiencing each morning before reporting to work. She found herself frequently calling in sick. The day finally came, when she resigned.

Action: Sitting at home Maria's anger escalated on a daily basis. She finally listened to her sister and sought legal counsel. Walking into the attorney's office, she wondered if she had a strong case. The first thing the female attorney said after listening to her story; "Yes, you do have a case." Even though Maria had made some major mistakes in dating the boss, she still had a right to file sexual harassment charges. She did, and she won.

Recourse: The legal action Maria proceeded with (with the help of her attorney) involved working in a hostile environment in which unwelcome conduct of a sexual nature created an uncomfortable, unbearable work environment.

Her boss gave Maria an option; "If you have dinner with me things around the office can be very nice, possible promotions and time off to travel. He also made it very clear, if she treated him good; he would give her some time off with pay.

Her recourse was proving "quid pro quo sexual harassment." Maria explained to her attorney, she was afraid of not cooperating with her boss for fear of losing her job. Maria explained that she desperately needed the income from the job.

Maria's attorney explained; the coworkers did not have any right making lewd sexual remarks in front of her desk, knowing that she was in earshot and could hear everything. The off-color jokes were also out of line, in accord with appropriate protocol in the work place. These two occurrences, constituted a "hostile environment." This type of environment, according to the law, can be created by many different employees, each making one or a few offensive statements. Individually, the statements might not be "severe or pervasive" enough to pose as a liability, but in the aggregate may prove actionable.

4

RELIGION IN THE OFFICE
"Linda's Story"

Descriptive Analysis: Workplace harassment in reference to the law extends far beyond slurs, vulgar sexual propositions and hardcore pornography. The EEOC reported, an employer allowed the daily broadcast of prayers over the public address system. The Commission felt this type of conduct, which extended over a year, was sufficient to allege the existence of a hostile work environment predicated on *religious discrimination*. A state court found *religious harassment* in the workplace, when an employer placed religious articles in the employee newsletter. This same employer also printed Christian verses on employee's paychecks.

Read Linda's story and decide for yourself, what type of discrimination or harassment did Linda experience?

Interview: Meet Linda, age 46, recent divorcee, no children. That is how Linda wanted to start the interview. She continued to say, what happened to her was one of the worse nightmares anyone could experience in a workplace.

As the nasty divorce was nearing the end, Linda knew she had to return to work in order to support the lifestyle she was accustomed. The divorce decree released Dave's responsibility of paying the bills, and Linda knew the little settlement she received was not going to last very long.

Before marrying Dave five years ago, Linda had a wonderful position as Marketing Director in a Fortune 500 firm. However, Dave insisted she resign and be available to travel with him. It sounded like the ideal life. Linda had not imagined how life could take a nasty turn when another woman entered the picture. She knew before the marriage Dave enjoyed the opposite sex, and had no qualms in doing what ever he wanted. The signs were there, when they first met, Dave was living with a woman. This did not stop him from approaching Linda for a date, even though he knew Linda was a married woman.

Dave proved to be quite the ladies man; Linda was the first to admit his charm was over whelming. After three months, Linda had divorced Alex her first husband and moved into the house where Dave used to share with his significant other. Things moved very fast, almost too fast. One month later, they were married.

"Surprise, surprise!" Linda chimed, "Their five-year anniversary arrived with Dave giving her notice that he wanted a divorce." Sitting there in total shock, all she could hear was Dave's voice off in a distance in his usual pontificating manner. He was pacing up and down the room exclaiming how wonderful it was, finding his true "soul mate."

The divorce did not take long, for there was not a lot of money to distribute. It was very simple; all the money was spent on trips, clothes and dining out every night. Linda said as she sighed: "I was a fool, an absolute fool. How could I have been so blind, and not have seen it coming?"

Linda continued the interview saying, she came to the realization that life goes on after the death of a marriage. One day after experiencing a few months of depression, she decided to do something about her situation. One interview after another came and went, but no job offers. She was starting to become desperate, when she interviewed at a small firm where they offered her a position, she grabbed it. Linda blatantly admitted, she had jumped in the water before testing the temperature.

Monday morning arrived and Linda feeling the excitement of the first day at work, walked into the office an hour early. The only person there was the janitor. The elderly man smiled and let her in the front door.

The day seemed to pass without any upsetting nuances. Before leaving for the evening, the office manager reminded Linda that every Tuesday morning at 7:00 am, there was a required staff meeting. Linda responded; "no problem, I will be there."

The next morning arrived; Linda seated herself in the conference room next to some of her co-workers. A few minutes elapsed when the CEO walked proudly into the room and stood at the head of the conference table. Then to Linda's astonishment, the CEO started a series of prayers in which the entire staff would yell "amen." This went on for an hour. Feeling uncomfortable, she was not quite sure what to do. Linda was the first to admit that she was not a deeply religious person. Pausing for a moment, Linda then turned and stared out the window. "You see, I am not religious as the definition goes, but I am spiritual." As an interviewer I quickly interjected: "Linda could you please explain the difference between being religious and spiritual?

"It is quite simple, I am not a firm believer in man-made religion and do not require a building where I report to in order to communicate with my Higher Power." Linda told me, she was raised in the Catholic religion, but through the years became frustrated with rules, if not obeyed, would condemn her to mortal damnation. She continued to say, she liked communicating with her Higher Power, using her own words and not mimicking rote that someone else wrote a thousand years ago. Linda nervously laughed and said, "Here she was, the second day of her job, literally thrown to the lions and being forced to pray in a rock of ages manner."

Tuesday arrived once again with its mandatory staff meeting. This time she decided, since she enjoyed her job, she would make the best of it and shout out the amens with the same type of gusto as her co-workers. Nevertheless, what happened next, made Linda sick to her stomach. It seems that one of the younger women in her department was ordered to stand at the end of the table and confess she had an affair with a guy in the office. To make matters worse, the guy was married, and now here she was standing in front of her co-workers, begging for their forgiveness. Only ten-minutes had elapsed when the young woman broke down and started sobbing. It seems that it was not only verboten to have an affair with a married man in this office, but to throw acid on the womb, she was pregnant. The saga never seemed to end. In the name of religion, the poor young woman was branded a sinner and probably emotionally scarred forever.

The CEO rose out of his seat and walked over to the young woman, gently putting his arm around her, telling her everything would be all right for the group will pray for her redemption. Linda admitted that the prayers she could handle, but not this type of witch-hunt.

As an interviewer, I could see Linda was becoming emotionally distraught, relating the story. I asked her if she wanted to take a break and continue the interview later. "No" she said, "I'll be ok."

Attempting to regain her composure, Linda started to giggle. I immediately asked her "What was so funny?" She said she had read a book many years ago on the subject of the Salem witch-hunts. One situation remained planted in her mind, when an individual in the community accused another person of being a witch. The criteria for judgment was; the accused would be thrown in the lake, if the poor soul drown, she was clearly not a witch, but if the person swam, it proved she was certainly a witch and would then be burned at the stake. Nothing like a two-edged sword with a no win situation.

Linda after discussing the problem with her best friend, decided she definitely liked the job and was afraid after being there two weeks, a resignation would not look good on her resume'. The next day she requested time to talk with the CEO of the company. If anyone could understand her feelings of course, he would. Linda was the first to admit her naivety.

John, the CEO was around fifty years old, with a balding head and an enormous protruding gut. When he saw Linda, a great big smile appeared on his face. This expression soon faded as Linda sat in front of his huge desk pouring out her feelings of discomfort as to the Tuesday morning revival staff meetings. John sat with a serious look on his face and took a long time to respond. "Well, little lady, it is obvious you just don't fit in. However, that's all right, I am going to tell you what I am going to do. I suggest that you skip the Tuesday meetings and then he quickly added, especially if it makes you uncomfortable."

He then smiled and stood up motioning her to the door. Linda jumped to her feet and let him escort her out of his office. She turned around to thank him for his understanding, but he had already returned to his office where he quickly closed the door.

The next two weeks turned into a nightmare. Linda's manager was constantly complaining her work was not the quality the company required. What irritated Linda was that before her little chitchat with the CEO, she received compliments as to her job performance. The worm had turned; Linda knew it was just a matter of time before she would be accused of being a witch.

The next week Linda had a pile of work on desk a mile high. No human in a lifetime would have been able to complete the work along with the time demands attached. Linda worked feverishly around the clock, even taking work home with her at night, but it eventually caught up with her. After three weeks, she had no choice, but to offer her letter of resignation.

Action: Linda did not contact an attorney until two months after the incident. Since she did not have substantial evidence, and had been at the company for such a short period, the attorney advised her not to bother filing charges. As a sidebar, the young woman that was forced to repent in the staff meeting now has pending charges with the EEOC.

Recourse: According to the rules set by the EEOC, Linda did have a case of religious harassment. and desperate treatment. A recent article reported that unwanted preaching in the workplace offending employees was actionable harassment. It was also reported by a federal district court that held a pattern of religiously themed comments, which mostly consisted of statements that focused on a sinner who had to repent, was substantial grounds for harassment. (as seen in this case)

This case may also have another type of *discrimination* and that is the employer's failure to make reasonable accommodation to an employee's religious beliefs. There are several laws, regulations, and court decisions that require and employer to refrain from discrimination on the basis of disability and religion. The employer is also required to take affirmative steps in order to accommodate those two factors.

Most cases of disparate treatment involve discharge or discipline. In this case, the employer intentionally treated the Linda differently than the other employees. The workload in Linda's story was agreed upon during the initial interview. After Linda's complaint the workload tripled and time requirements shortened. None of Linda's coworkers was given extra work with tight time requirements

In *disparate treatment cases*, an individual must initially prove a *prima facie* case based on *retaliatory treatment*. To establish a *prima facie* case of retaliation, the individual must show the following:

1. The individual is in a protected activity that is recognized by the employer

2. An *adverse employment action* occurred

3. There is some form of a casual connection between the above two…

The definition of casual connection may fall under the categories of:

1. An *adverse employment action* (assigning amounts of work that are impossible to complete in the given time)

2. Demotion

3. Termination

5

NEPOTISM
"Sydney's Story"

Descriptive Analysis: The definition of *Nepotism* entails perceptions of favoritism in the workplace. This often occurs when relatives or spouses work together for the same employer. For example: the CEO owns the company and hires Jimmy (his son) to be Vice President, Jody (his daughter) to be CFO, with Jody's husband acting COO.

Interview: The interview series would not be complete without someone representing the bean counters of the world. Meet Sydney or Sid, as she prefers to be called, our in-house accountant. "People always ask me about my name. I guess my dad always wanted a boy, you see I have a body that could easily pass for a tight end on a football team."

Being born in the sixties, Sid attended high school where it was common knowledge, the boys played the sports and the girls stood giggling on the side as they jumped up and down in uncoordinated cheerleading type movements. Plopping down in an over stuffed chair, I knew Sid was ready to start the interview: "Oh well, enough of the past, let's get going."

Sid's career started in the early seventies when she graduated with an accounting degree from the University of Illinois. After graduation, the next step in building her career was to interview with an accounting firm. The first three years Sid worked as a gopher, laughing as she reminisced, "All I did was go for this and go for that." Still laughing, she said she thought she had majored in culinary arts; her primary job each noon was to pick-up lunch orders. The only time I saw any numbers was during tax season, then they worked me like a dog, almost twenty hours a day.

Meanwhile Sid's career was advancing, she dated and married Arthur a promising lawyer. After four kids, a dog and two cars in the garage, Sid thought it was time to get back into the real world of making money. Being out of the industry for twenty-one years, she felt it was necessary to hone her abilities by taking a few review courses. After six months and completion of the courses, she aggressively attacked the market and landed a job with a mom and pop small manufacturing company. Everything seemed to go well for the first year, and then things started to fall apart. Sid realized that something was wrong when numerous accounting irregularities were appearing on her desk. The numbers seemed to be manipulated and not accurately reflecting the employee's performances. Each week at the general meeting, management and the lead dog in the accounting department would pass out the weekly financial reports. Sid realized the numbers were not jiving with the actuals, resulting in employees not being paid their fare share.

Not quite sure what to do, Sid did feel she had to discuss this problem with someone, but whom? The president of the company was the owner's son, the VP was the son-in-law, and finally yet importantly the head accountant was a first cousin. Nothing like a quintessential paradigm of a classic case of nepotism. Sid knew if she uncovered the problem, her head would roll. The company's matrix was structured in such a way, anyone with half a brain could surmise who the survivors would be if the ship were sinking.

Looking at me, Sid asked if she could tell me something that was strictly her opinion, or did she have to stick mainly with definitive facts? I responded, "No, by all means tell me how you feel."

During each Friday departmental meeting, the president (who everyone chidingly referred to as Jr.) would constantly remind the employees as to how poorly the company was performing financially. At one meeting in particular, and to the amazement of the staff, he likened the company to the Titanic.

Each week Jr. would berate some poor individual and blame him or her for the week's short coming. During the last meeting, one of the bookkeepers fled the room in tears, and the operations director slammed out in disgust. This was not a surprise to any of us, it was a weekly occurrence.

A few months went by and the company was quickly approaching the Christmas season. The first week of December, the staff meeting was held at its usual time on Friday. Sid laughed and said that was when she received an unexpected Christmas present. "I guess it was my turn for the wrath of the president to come down on my head." In the middle of the meeting, Jr. turned towards Sid and made the comment, it seems someone had accidentally found a few problems and was spreading unjustifiable rumors around the office, trying to destroy employee morale. "Why he looked at me, I don't know. All I did was make a passing comment to one of my colleagues, as how I thought the situation should be remedied."

After the meeting, Jr. requested my presence in his office. When I arrived, I was not surprised to see the Spanish Inquisition. Present at the meeting was Jr, the VP, and last but not least, the head accountant. Jr was the first to speak. He asked me straight out, what was the problem. I turned towards him after glancing at the other two, whom by the way were both staring at the ground, and replied that I noticed a few accounting irregularities that I felt should be addressed. Jr. stood up and shouted at me that it was none of my business and that I should quit my female meddling. Sid thought to herself, I have nothing to lose, so she stood up and faced Jr directly and said: " I have a feeling that I had better resign for you will find something to fire me over, won't you?" Jr. with a sickly looking grin on his face replied: "You bet your sweet little ass I will, and guess what honey, I have witnesses as to your actions today in this meeting, right boys?"

Sid turned and walked out of the room, slamming the door behind her. She knew she really did not have any recourse, but to voluntarily resign. The first thing to do was to call Arthur at his office and explain what happened. One nice thing about being married to an attorney, no legal fees.

Like usual, Arthur put Sid on hold for a moment and then returned to say he now could talk. Sid blurted out every little detail of what had taken place at the company. After a long pause, Arthur started to list legal reasons that were not in her best interest. First of all, remember when you wanted to work for that company and I told you to beware for it was run by the family? Sid knew Arthur was right, but darn she thought, did he always have to be right? Arthur continued to say, she could take legal recourse but it would be a long drawn out process and in the end produce very few results. "You have to remember Sid, blood is thicker than water. Families stick together, especially if there is a familial pecking order, in which livelihoods are on the line. Isn't it obvious? Sid it may be time to move on with your career, consider the job as an entry back into the industry, and leave it at that."

Action: Two months later, after Arthur helped her revise her resume', Sid signed on with a small local accounting firm. Even though she had always wanted to work for a big firm, she was realistic. Sid knew her age was against her, especially when it came to the big firms. The word on the street was the big firms tended to hire new entrants right out of college, not married, and of course no responsibilities with children.

Recourse: There is not a lot an individual can do when the company is owned and financed by one person, and that person's first loyalty is to his/her family. Understand the situation before accepting the job.

Suggestion: To avoid difficulties down the road, when establishing the employment contract try to specify the parameters. It is difficult, but find out what the rules of the game are before the play begins. How to do this, sometimes the only way is to ask permission to spend a little time in the office before signing on. One or two days is not going to show you where the skeletons are hid, and in what closet. However, if you are intuitive, you may pick up a few subtle, unspoken nuances that may offer you a clue or clues as to what the company's dynamics are.

6

ABUSE AT WORK & ABUSE AT HOME
"Ora's Story"

Descriptive Analysis: This interview was selected to illustrate that a situation can involve more than one type of *discrimination*. The interviewee had a right to file for *racial, gender,* and *religious discrimination*.

Nobody wants to be treated unfairly, but sometimes it happens. *Anti-discrimination* legislation makes it easier for individuals to get a fair chance by providing information in concern with rights and responsibilities, as well as, establishing processes for filing a complaint about *discrimination* and their resolutions.

The only type of *discrimination* not yet explained in this book is *racial discrimination*. This type of discrimination occurs when an individual is treated unfairly compared to others due to their race, color, descent, or national-ethnic origin. Legislation has been enacted in the case of racial or religious hostility or hatred. A lawful protectorate is titled, Anti-discrimination legislation. This refers to the rights of individuals obtaining a fair chance regardless of their characteristics and in deference to unfair attitudes and practices.

See if you as the reader can identify the areas of *discrimination* (mentioned above) in the following interview.

Interview: A beautiful black woman from Trinidad, with short-cropped hair and incredibly perfect teeth sat across from me during the next interview. Ora, being fifty-four years of age, did not have one wrinkle on her face. When she smiled, her entire face lit up with a super healthy glow. I could not help myself as the interviewer, but I had to ask how she maintained the youthful image? Ora looked at me and smiled, "you see I have a good gene pool, if you saw my ninety year old mother, you wouldn't guess her to be a day over sixty. Also I truly believe in mind over matter, what I mean is having a good attitude and laughing a lot will miraculously keep the years off." "Now" Ora said, "If you get me started, I will pontificate for hours as to the virtues of healthy bodies and minds, and then she laughingly added, "We will never get to the interview."

Ora started the interview by saying, "I guess I stayed in the job longer than what I should have, and it was truly unbearable at times. She continued to say; she not only loved her job, but also wanted to prove to her husband that she could be successful. The first reason for remaining in the job was sensible, but the second reason, was complete unmitigated stupidity. "My husband had no idea of what I was experiencing at work, the humiliation and the subtle, but hostile daily remarks. Now recalling the last year, I don't think my husband really cared."

Ora said, she was aware before accepting the job; the club had a high turn over in the Athletic Director's position. She knew being a woman and being black, was not going to be easy. Then she thought, this is not the sixties where Blacks had to sit in the back of the bus. "How naïve I was in thinking, racial discrimination as part of the past."

"Ok, let's start at the beginning." You see the Club Manager decided all middle management had to accept the responsibilities of "Manger on Duty" (M.O.D.) It was simply that an employee had to complete his or her daily-managerial requirements, then an additional six more hours, on assigned days.

The Athletic club business requires staying open for extremely long hours, in this case the club opened at 5:30 am and closed at 11:00 pm. During the day, the first shift opens the club at 5:30 am, the second shift starts at 11:00 am and continues to 5:00 pm where the third shift starts and continues until the 11:00 o'clock closing. The director of the maintenance department always volunteered for the opening shift. This gesture was not pure of heart, for he his job description stated that had to report to the club at 5:30 am.

The general manager's favorite individuals were assigned the fluff position at 11:00 am and individuals the general manager wanted to give a hard time received the closing shifts. The fluff position was a no-action MOD role. The assigned individual could work their respective job and at the same time complete this additional requirement. This was a no-brainer shift, nothing had to be done by the individual, except be there. The closing shift was difficult, it encompassed cleaning the swimming pool area, closing out the registers, locking and setting alarm systems, and requesting members to leave.

After being out of the industry for ten years, Ora realized re-entering the business arena where she left was going to be difficult, especially in the small city where they had moved. "But I was ready to bite the bullet and do what it took to get back into the industry. But cleaning lavatories, and picking up dirty towels late at night, proved to be more difficult than I expected."

Ora explained, the Athletic Director's position entailed being at the club sometimes early in the morning, which resulted in a fourteen hour, non-stop day. She continued to say; she did not have set hours. The Athletic Director assigned Ora the responsibility of over-seeing 60 employees. The majority of these people were part-time employees, which meant, they came and went at different times. "In order to touch base with these people, I had to be there at the hours they were working." The majority of these employees had primary jobs, using the club as a secondary job entitled them to have full use the club's facilities. "In order to be effective, I had to be there at a variety of different hours. "I really did not mind, for I knew communication with 'all' of my staff was crucial to the success of the program. Unfortunately, management's attitude did not coincide with my beliefs of how to operate successful programs."

Ten months passed and Ora was finding it extremely difficult to perform her duties and her assigned MOD times. She thought if she could discuss the times with the manager, something could be worked out. "I just wanted to explain to him, the hours were killing me. If he wanted me to do a professional job, then he had to understand, I needed a different time schedule.

Ora thought her request was reasonable and explained that she was not trying to get out of work, but felt she could be more effective not having to perform as many of the night closing MOD responsibilities that were presently assigned. She started too say, "I already put in over sixty hours a week, and this is not counting the extra responsibilities." Just as she started another sentence, the manager stopped her in her tracks. Ora said, she was completely thrown off guard when the manager looked at her sternly and said; "don't pull that, you think just because you are a woman and black, that you can come in here and demand certain privileges. "Well forget it. You have to work the hours I assign you, otherwise go find another job." In an apologetic tone, Ora replied, "I am sorry if I have offended you, that was not the reason for meeting with you. I just thought you would understand and be willing to help me. Before the meeting, I figured out how we could work this out. I don't mind the MOD assignments, but was wondering if I could have one or two of the mid-day times. This would lessen some of the hours.

The manager was shocked that Ora had the nerve to continue the conversation. "Listen, I feel it is best for the club that you work the late night shift, and that is that, no more conversation."

Ora felt her hands were tied; the meeting with the general manager was behind closed doors without any witnesses to attest as to the manager's abusive manner. Ora was afraid that anything she said, would be turned around and used against her. Quietly and calmly, she turned towards the manager and thanked him for his time. She then stood up and calmly walked out of the office.

After the meeting, things became even worse. It was common knowledge around the club that Ora placed a high degree of importance on attending Catholic Mass every Sunday with her family. When the next MOD schedule was posted, Ora not only was assigned all the late night shifts, but also Saturday evenings and Sunday mornings shifts. That night when she told her husband, he became violently angry and screamed at her "Why don't you do something about this, you probably just sat there like a wimp and took his abuse. Now he is getting back at you, and guess what, you deserve it, you're the most cowardly piece of work I ever met." With tears in her eyes she explained, "I tried really hard to do a professional job, and I know I did." It is just the situation of working sixty plus hours a week, with the extra responsibilities. Her husband started shaking his fist at her screaming, "you think you are a professional, huh! you deserve to pick up dirty towels at night. "That's what a black woman like you deserve." He then slammed the door and drove off.

Ora did not see her husband for the next two days, and did not question him when he returned. She looked at me and said in a sullen tone, "I know I should care, he's my husband and the father of my children, but I was glad when he left."

The next day Ora decided she had to approach the general manager, in some way, about the Sunday situation. There was no way she was going to arrange another face to face meeting with him. Instead, she decided to send him a memo. The memo started by asking if there was a mistake in the schedule, for she never had been scheduled to work on Sundays in the past. A day later, she received a reply. There is no mistake in the scheduling of the days; all employees must conform accordingly. Remember, no one gets special privileges around here.

Months passed, and the level of grief and frustration increased on a daily basis. Lowering her voice and staring out the window, Ora said, "I just didn't want to give up."

Between work and home, Ora admitted, "At times I thought I was losing it." The abuse at home did not stop, but escalated with her husband making more demands that conflicted with her work. It was insane, Ora said, "He wanted me to work, I know for a fact he liked the paycheck. I just could not understand why he constantly set up obstacles to make life more difficult for me."

Six months later, Ora called me and announced, "It's over, I am pleased too say, you are talking to a divorced woman." Ora explained she grew tired of trying to please her husband and the manager of the club. She made the decision one day, no more abuse from either of them.

Ora is now writing children's books and has a wonderful relationship with her agent. She said, "I thank God each and every Sunday, that I got out of not one, but two bad situations."

Action: Ora talked with a female attorney she had met at the Club. After hearing Ora's story, the attorney informed her as to possible charges to be filed. Charges of discrimination covering race, gender, and religion.

The attorney proceeded to say, the manager insinuated that just because you are black and a woman, you feel you deserve extra perks. That was his first mistake. In reference to the religious discrimination, you had set a precedent by attending Sunday mass each week. Only after the confrontation in the manager's office, did the scheduling for MOD responsibilities change.

Ora went through mediation, but did not find satisfactory results and is now proceeding to a jury trial. She said she felt extremely fortunate having a professional attorney that agreed to handle her case on a contingency basis. The case at this time, is still pending

Recourse: The charges filed were:

1. Racial discrimination (manger's racial slurs)

2. Gender discrimination (manger's reference to her being a woman)

3. Religious discrimination (after the conflict occurred, the change in her work days to include Sunday, especially after a precedent had been set in the past as to working on this day)

4. Disparate Treatment (demanding in order to keep her job she had to work the undesirable shifts)

7

PROMOTION DENIED
"Judy's Story"

Descriptive Analysis: Unfortunately in the year 2000, the "*good ole boy system*" prevails in the workplace. A perfect example of this discrimination is best illustrated through the story of an older former-football coach that is now running a company. This man's theory is that if you want something done right then give it to a male counter part, otherwise it will not be accomplished. The woman's place is in the home, where her main responsibility is to take care of the children and her husband. Moreover, if a woman has to work for a living, then the menial jobs are appropriate. Females have to remember that this is a man's world, and they have no choice but accept their place.

According to the society of Human Resource Management (SHRM) "Barriers to Advancement Survey" conducted in 1999, old fashion attitudes still prevail in the workplace. The survey reported that corporate cultures still favor men. There are perceptions that women are more likely to quit for family reasons. This type of thinking prevents women from rising in the corporate ranks. Tory Johnson, founder and chief executive officer of New York based Women for Hire, reported there are only two female CEOs in the Fortune 500 companies.

Usually the football coach turned company director scenario is seen as being a little more subtle in today's workplace environment. Nevertheless, there still exists an unwritten code, which holds that one has a better chance of succeeding, if he or she is a member of the "good ole boy system." The sometimes unspoken attitude is; men don't expect a female's ability to be able to keep up with their male counterpart. Subtle

---

*The Wall Street Journal (10-17-2000). <u>Cultural Conflict: Women and Minorities continue to Take a Backseat in Business.</u> Recruitment Diversity career journal.com.

Interview: Judy, a petite framed, green eyed, brunette, sat across from me during the interview and poured out her heart as to how the good ole boy system got the best of her. It seems she had been employed by a firm for the last ten years, slowly working her way up the corporate ladder. She worked long hours and never complained about therequiredextensive travel.

Judy admitted that making the choice to return to work created a hardship on her marriage. However, for some reason, thank heavens, even with the traveling her marriage prevailed. Charlie accepted the sacrifices that Judy had to make in order to accomplish her goals. He had been in corporate America for twenty-five years rising from sales to a CEO position. Judy stuck with him through the hard times so he felt reciprocity was in order. Never thinking that when he turned fifty-five he would be offered a golden parachute and an early retirement. Charlie decided to take the retirement offer and now found himself reversing roles with Judy. It helped that the three kids were off to college. Judy sighed and expressed how impossible it would have been with Charlie in charge of the household.

Judy, in her mid-forties, thought she had a chance of going somewhere in a corporation. With a smile on her face and a twinkle in her eyes, she proudly announced that she had the energy of a sixteen year old.

A computer company advertised in the newspaper of an immediate job opening for someone with strong managerial skills. Judy interviewed, and was offered the job, which she immediately accepted. Working in a technology-based company proved to be challenging but exciting at the same time. Things were constantly changing, not from day to day, but from minute to minute. She admitted that having a logical mind definitely helped when working with 'techies' (computer professionals). It would have been great if the director of the company had similar attitudes, as did the computer nerds. Unfortunately, he viewed the world as a man's domain, in which the male counter-part ruled as king. It was interesting to watch him when he entered the office each day. The first place he would visit was the sales department. After 'shooting the breeze' as he called it, he would then saunter around to the mid-management office support area, run by ninety-five percent women. It never failed, each time he would begin with a story about one of his grandchildren. Before leaving, he would ask each female employee, how her family life was going? How are the kids? And, did anyone need help from the sales/management department?

One day when the company's director entered the front door, Judy was actively attempting to solve a problem with the help from a colleague. Noticing that he was standing in the doorway, Judy exchanged the common courtesies and continued with her conversation. About a minute later, she noticed he was still standing in the entrance. Realizing that he was listening intently to the conversation, Judy immediately invited him to join in. "Please feel free to offer any suggestions."

The next thing that happened almost knocked her off her feet. The director looked at Judy and told her not to be concerned with the problem, one of his sales managers would handle it. Then proceeded to ask Judy, if she could get him a cup of coffee.

When Judy first started working for the company, Marsha was the assigned supervisor of her division. Marsha was fortunate; she received the supervisory promotion from the former Company's director. She was firmly established in this position before the present director arrived.

Over the last two months, Judy noticed Marsha was starting to slack off. She would call in sick at least twice a week, or not show up for work at all. Everyone knew she would be eventually fired. The day finally came. The director arrived early one morning and after a ten-minute meeting, Marsha was seen cleaning out her desk and quietly leaving through the side door.

Around noon, all employees were requested to meet in the cafeteria. Word travels fast in a small environment, and everyone knew the director was going to make the announcement of the supervisor's dismissal. In the meantime, the director announced two men; both in their mid-twenties would assume the office responsibilities until a replacement was found. One of the guys was the comptroller and the other one was a dispatch manager. Neither one had a clue of how to operate and manage an office.

The director then proceeded to announce that anyone interested in interviewing for the open position should see him immediately. No one came forward, except for Judy. The director looked at her sternly, and commented that he really was not surprised for after observing her for the last couple of months, knew she wanted the position. Judy, ignoring the way the director responded, quickly reminded him that she had previous extensive experience in this type of position. The only reason she accepted a lower level job, was that the assistant manager's job was the only available position open at the time. Judy proceeded to explain to the director that she had been hoping and waiting for this opportunity.

Two weeks passed after Judy's request for an interview with the director. Another week elapsed with still no scheduled time for an interview. When Judy saw the director in the hallway, she would politely nod her head and say 'hello', but would not receive an acknowledgement in return. At first when she told Charlie of how she was being treated since she submitted her name for the manager's position, he would respnd by saying that she was simply acting paranoid. Right, Judy thought, even a complete idiot could realize when he or she was being treated differently. It seemed as though, almost over night, she had contracted leprosy, or something equally distasteful.

One day as Judy was on her way to have lunch with a friend, the receptionist stopped her and informed her that the director wanted to see her in his office, "a.s.a.p." As Judy walked up the long staircase and entered the office, she speculated as to what was on the director's mind. Maybe he was finally going to arrange an interview time. The director motioned her to come in and sit down. "Ok, he said, let's start your interview." Taken back by surprise, Judy commented that she preferred to have sufficient preparation before walking into an interview.

The director, in a snappy retort, said if she wanted an interview it had to be now or never, "So what's it going to be lady?" Judy knew what he meant by the tone he used when he called her lady. She quietly nodded her head in an affirmative manner, sat back in the over-sized leather chair, waiting for a barrage of questions to fly. The interview included typical, run of the mill every day questions. The type of questions that were difficult to respond in an intelligent manner.

About fifty-minutes elapsed when Judy noticed the director looking nervously at his watch. She wasalmost tempted to say something, but decided it was not a good idea or the right time. Five minutes went by and once again, Judy saw him glancing impatiently at his watch.

At the end of the hour, just as the clock struck one, the director stated that the interview was officially over. Judy knew that the entire interview was pure fluff without any substance. Throughout the interview, Judy felt like the director was simply placating her by conducting the obligatory interview.

When the director stated the interview was concluded, Judy knew exactly were she stood. She had suspected foul play before entering his office. Judy said, she had no idea what got into to her, but felt the hair on the back of her neck stand up. As she rose to her feet, she turned towards the director and said: "I don't have a chance of getting this position, you're merely going through the motions." She then turned with what little dignity she could garner marched out of the director's office. Tears came swelling in her eyes, trying desperately to hold them back, Judy walked briskly out the company's front door. Oh God she thought, people are looking and staring at me, but you know what, for the first time in my life, I don't care. That night Charlie held Judy as she softly cried herself to sleep.

Judy called in ill the next two days. She admitted that she had a tough time pulling herself together after such a travesty of injustice, blatant rudeness, and humiliation. Charlie was wonderful and was always there to listen when she needed to vent. The third day arrived when she got up early in the morning and announced to Charlie that she was going to fight the company 'tooth and nail." Charlie's response was: "Go girl" and that is exactly what she did…all the way to a jury trial.

Action: The first thing Judy did was to contact one of her best friends; one that she knew had filed a *discrimination charge* a year ago. Her friend helped her find the appropriate law firm and what specific lawyer to use in the firm. She also questioned her friend regarding legal fees.

After arriving at the law offices of Brickman and Daily, Judy was escorted by the receptionist to a large conference room. This is where she met Bill, soon to be her legal counsel and eventually one of her closest friends. She knew immediately that Bill was the right person. According to Judy, it was a gut feeling. After relating her story, he turned towards Judy and stated that he only took cases that he felt assured of winning. Judy's stomach performed a flip-flop, wondering if he considered her case to have what the pros call, merit. Bill started to laugh when he saw the look on Judy's face, and quickly told her to relax for he felt she had a *prima fascia* case, and one he would be honored to represent. As to the legal fees, Bill felt that ten-percent of the settlement would cover his time and expenses.

The next step for Judy was to set up a three-hour or more meeting with Bill, during which time they would lay out a plan of action. Meanwhile, Bill's office would draw up the proper paper work in order to file a claim with the *Equal Employment Opportunity Commission (EEOC)*. He explained EEOC's strict time frames had to be strictly adhered to. Bill softly assured Judy that his office would mange the time lines.

Next, Bill requested any type of paper trail that Judy had kept during her time of employment. This was easy for Judy, for she was taught years ago when typewriters were used, to keep an activity log and send appropriate dated memos. Bill was impressed with the paper documentation that Judy presented. It told the entire story, starting with the pre-dating of her employment at the company. Charlie had been the one to explain to Judy that if she ever (in her career) had to go to court, a paper trail documenting every situation would be critically important. This documentation should be written for the common person (juror) to be able to read and comprehend.

In the last hour of their meeting, Bill reassured Judy that she no longer had to deal with the director and the good ole boy system he represented. The next time Judy would probably encounter the director was either at mediation or in court. Knowing a little bit about the director, Bill said he would probably send in one of his managers to represent him and the company. Judy was relieved to hear this, for her nerves were already frayed. She told Charlie; " I didn't know how much more I could take.

The mediation process was the first option presented to Judy. Charlie had reminded her several times that if there was another way to resolve the conflict, she should do it. The last thing anyone wanted to do was to litigate and end up in court. Judy knew the mediation option would be less formal than going into court. Bill advised her to at least "give it a go." Therefore, Judy entered into *mediation,* but not without being prepared. Bill explained the emotional and psychological nuances she could possibly experience. He taught her how to stay calm. as calm as anyone can be under the circumstances.

Bill knew from his very short relationship with Judy that he needed to manage her expectations and spell out everything well in advance. He started by explaining that mediation involved both parties coming together to try to work things out. A neutral trained mediator (third person) would be there to help the process along. This person's job is to assist both sides evaluate their goals and options and move them in the direction of achieving a mutually satisfactory solution. Because the mediator does not have the authority to impose a decision, a result will not be reached unless both parties agree.

When the *mediation* begins, the mediator will introduce everyone and explain the rules and goals. He will continue on saying that he hopes each party involved works cooperatively toward reaching a fair settlement.

Next, each party is invited to explain in his/her own words what the problem entails and how he/she has been emotionally and psychologically affected. Each party has the opportunity to present ideas as to how he/she feels the situation can be resolved. Bill added, when one party is talking, the other party is not allowed to interrupt.

The *mediator* then encourages the parties to address the issues. As the mediation continues, the parties adjourn to separate private meeting rooms. Bill explained that the mediator will meet with us in this room in order to discuss what we feel are our strengths and weaknesses. This will be the time when we can discuss the possibilities of a *settlement.* After we finish with the mediator, he will join the opposing side and discuss the points we made with our suggestion(s) for a settlement. It's like the game of ping-pong. The *mediator* bounces back and forth between the two rooms negotiating with each side.

Sometimes after the negotiations conclude, the mediator will bring both sides back together to discuss any points that are still left unsettled. If a settlement is agreed upon in the individual meeting rooms, both parties may leave without coming back together.

At the end of the process, the mediator may sometimes detail the main provisions in writing, as both parties listen. The *mediator* may request both parties to sign the written summary of agreement. He may also suggest that the parties involved should have legal counsel conduct a review of the document.

If an agreement has not been reached for whatever reason(s), the mediator will advise every one of their options. Options afforded may include; meeting once again, entering into arbitration, or electing litigation and going to court.

Judy felt prepared when she walked into the *mediation.* After going through the steps exactly the way Bill had described, she felt a surge of confidence in her conviction. She was then asked by the mediator what she felt was a justified financial *settlement.* What Judy felt was fair, was like the difference between night and day. Judy and Bill nodded to each other confirming as to the type of mentality they were dealing with. Without any hesitation, they abruptly stood up and walked out.

On the way back to Bill's office, he asked her where she wanted to go from here. Judy stopped for a moment, then turned and looked Bill straight in the eyes and asked: "Do I have a good case? How else can I achieve my goal now that mediation has failed, or do I have to go through arbitration? " After this experience, I really do not relish the idea of a third party arbitrator making a final decision. I think in view of dealing with the good ole boy system mentality, I would have a much better chance in a court of law with a group of my peers (jurors). At least the jury will have a certain percentage of female representation.

Judy kept talking aloud. It was as though she was having a conversation with herself. Bill did not interrupt, but patiently waited for her to finish. "Ok, Judy said, "Let's shoot straight arrows here." Based on the assumption that a lawsuit is my best option, do you think I can win? Bill, without any type of hesitation replied, "Yes."

Before going further, Bill wanted Judy to answer a critical question. "How much is it worth to you to spend time and aggravation of going to *court?*" He then suggested that Judy place a dollar value on an hour of her time. She could then multiply that number by the number of hours Bill would estimate going to court would entail. "All right Judy, do you still want to sue?" In a split second, Judy responded, "Yes."

During the past two years, Judy had been accused of numerous things, ranging from lying under oath to stealing from the company. The company tried to dig up any dirt they could, then escalate it to incredible proportions. At times Bill thought Judy was going to throw in the towel, but to his amazement, her tenacity won out.

Two years and twenty-nine days later, after incessant subtle annoyances from the company she had brought charges against, Judy received the verdict. It was in her favor! Thinking back over the two years and of course not forgetting the twenty-nine days, I asked Judy if it was all worth it. Her response was: "yes...definitely yes." The award was not as much as Judy would have liked, but she felt good that justice was served.

What hurt more than anything, Judy said, was that certain 'friends' at the company, or at least she thought were friends, had lied under oath. Coming up with stories that were so bent out of shape, even she was amazed at times. These were people she had confided in, had lunch with, gone out with socially, and even sent presents to their children at Christmas. That really hurt.

Sitting in the courtroom hearing people tell the jury what a deceitful and mean person she was, hurt. It was amazing how they distorted the truth. The opposing attorney, who Judy admitted was very good at her job, only allowed her to answer questions with a yes or no, when an explanation was really needed for clarification.

Without Charlie's support, Judy said she would have given up. When she hit a low, he was there to pick her up and encourage her to keep going. Bill and his weird humor brought a laugh to Judy at the weirdest times. He lessened the stress by having Judy picture how stupid people really are. When Judy was being *deposed*, Charlie told her to picture the opposing attorney sitting at the end of the table in heart laced boxer shorts. "I know it sounds crazy, but things like that helped."

The company tried desperately to make Judy a liar. They flew in several women from within the company that were willing to testify that they were offered the position, but for some reason had to turn it down. Coincidentally, each woman just happened to be over the age of forty, and had deep ties in the part of the country where they resided. The majority of the women had jobs they were perfectly happy with along with husbands that were deeply entrenched in local businesses. What a laugh. It was common knowledge that they were pressuring other employees to testify with fabricated offers.

They went to every length to characterize Judy as an angry, unprofessional woman that merely wanted revenge. They described her as a person that was not aging gracefully and resented younger talent taking her place. Judy knew this was far from the truth, but there were times she admitted that she was not sure if she could continue. The final settlement was fair, Bill was pleased, and Judy felt a sense of accomplishment, in not letting the "good ole boy system" get the best of her.

Sidebar: The company's director unprofessional handling of Judy's work situation was one of the reasons for the company losing the case. Corporate was not pleased in the way he handled the negotiations and six months later, he was asked to resign.

Action: At the end of each interview, action(s) taken by the interviewee are described. In Judy's case, the last part of her interview described in detail for the reader (than what is usually portrayed here) as to what actions she pursued.

Recourse: The best course of action for an individual in this type of situation is to set feelings of rejection aside. Do not belabor the point of why the person who received the position is un-qualified. Instead, take a positive stance, and research how it would be possible to get ahead and move to another position, or another company.

If the individual feels there is a *case* of *discrimination*, then the first thing to do is check the employee's handbook as to specific policies. These policies usually clarify job requirements and position qualifications. Secondly, produce a file including the individual's performance reviews. If he or she received high marks, then this documentation would support the filing of charge(s). Thirdly, a meeting with the human resource representative may prove beneficial. At this meeting, the individual may express concerns and request answers. If all this fails, then the individual may file a charge with the *Equal Employment Opportunity Commission (EEOC)*.

The individual may elect to file a complaint with the state that enforces the fair employment laws (must be a resident of the state). If an agency decides to investigate the complaint, a request to the employer must be made as to the reason(s) the position was not offered to the charging individual.

8

SEXUAL INFLUENCE IN THE WORK PLACE
"Samantha's Story"

Descriptive Analysis: Over time women have learned the nuances involved, and have developed certain ways to act in order to use their femininity to the maximum. There is no law against women manipulating men for their own use. Throughout history, women have proven to be very successful manipulators. Look at Cleopatra, Tokyo Rose, just too mention a few. Intelligent women can use their bodies and minds effectively in a "man's world."

This next interview is very different from the others already presented in this book. There are two interviews, one with Samantha, a street-smart woman that knows how to play the game for her own benefit, and the other interview involves her former husband and his infidelity.

Interview: When I sat down with Samantha, who prefers to be called Sam, I saw a bubbly, Dallas type cheerleader sitting in front of me. Sam was thirty-eight years old when I conducted the interview with her.

In her third year of high school, Sam met Jimmy and fell madly in love. She did not complete her senior year for she was pregnant with their first child. Sam looked me straight in the eyes and told me that was the worst mistake of her life, which she still is paying for now. Then she added, her concept of life was that when you were given a lemon, it was your job to make lemonade.

Now comes the critical part of the interview. Sam is now in the process of a divorce with Jimmy. The question is how is she going to support her five kids, ranging from two-years to nineteen years old. In the last few years, Jimmy started to have trouble at the office where he was employed and started drinking quite heavily. Sometimes Sam did not see him for days. The day arrived when Sam admitted that she could no longer continue with life the way it was going. Even though Jimmy insisted that she stay at home and take care of the house and the kids.

She knew that she was at the point where she could no longer count on him.

At the time of the interview, she was teaching in a day care center. This was perfect; Sam could take three of her children with her to work without paying for a babysitter. The center was owned by a fifty-nine old man, who had the reputation of not being able to keep his hands off his employees. Sam had heard the rumors, but did not care, she was grateful to have landed a job.

The owner of the center had a young manager that conducted the day-to-day business. This guy had the I.Q. of about seventy. Sam knew her position would be solid if she played along with the young guy and smiled at the owner when he visited the center. On those days when the owner was scheduled to visit, she knew exactly how to dress and wear her hair. It worked. The hardest part was appearing to be super busy when either one of the 'good ole boys' were around.

The first year passed by quickly. The owner was pleased with her job performance and gave her excellent reviews. Sam was soon promoted to the assistant director of the center. She was excited that she was moving up the managerial line. All she had to do was to play the game. And she did.

Sam openly admitted without any qualms that she was ready to do what ever it took and prayed daily that she would not have to sacrifice her morals. According to Sam, the key to success was in knowing how far to take the flirtations, and when to exit before she got into a real uncompromising position. Sam was always teetering on the edge. Her story is of someone who was lucky, and skillful enough to be able to play the game without being caught.

Sam and I (interviewer) realized that her experiences in the work-place were not of a true problematic nature. She had volunteered to be part of the study, because of her problems at work fending off the owner and the manager. After extensive consideration, I made the deci-sion to keep her story in the book. The reasoning for the interview inclusion was predicated on the fact; her experiences were true to the workplace environment. Many women go through the same type of situations Sam related in her interview.

After the interview, Sam and I sat and talked about life in general. During the conversation, I realized Sam did have a story to tell, even though it was from a third person's perspective. Here is Sam's story as it pertains to the subject of the book.

A few years ago, Sam lived through the agony of her husband's infidelity. Jimmy committed the number workplace in digression, having an affair at the office. After management found out about the affair, the relationship was quickly curtailed. Both parties were immediately ordered, not to have any contact with each other. The "other woman" refused to abide with the managerial directive, and continued to contact Jimmy through different departmental secretaries. According to Jimmy, he refused the delivery of any of the correspondence. The "other woman" then tried contacting him by phone. He said he never returned any of her calls. One day Jimmy approached "the other woman" in the office and asked her implicitly to stop calling.

What happened next led to Jimmy's downfall. The "other woman" gossiped around the office about the affair. Finally, in total desperation, Jimmy set up a meeting with the department supervisor. At the meeting, he explained what the current situation was in the office. Instead of leaving it at that, he demanded that the "other woman' be fired.

Management frowned not only on infidelity type affairs in the office, but also at employee's making demands. This type of employee behavior was totally unacceptable. What happened next was to be expected, but not by Jimmy. Before the end of the day, Jimmy and the "other woman" were immediately terminated, and requested to leave the company's premise a.s.a.p. The company's attitude was that they could not co-exist in the same office and it would be blatantly unfair not to fire one, and not to fire the other

Jimmy told Sam that night, he felt he had been wrongfully terminated. The next day, he sought legal advice. The attorney listened patiently to Jimmy while he ranted and raved about how he was mis-treated. After about an hour, the attorney informed Jimmy that he would not accept the case, for he felt it was without merit. Jimmy screwed up, and now he has to pay the price. The first mistake and major mistake Jimmy made was that he did not make the argument that the "other woman" could be considered a pest. This would have validated terms for harassment in the workplace.

The fact that Jimmy and the "other woman" were formerly involved on a romantic basis, further complicated matters. The company's pol-icy clearly stated the requirements employees had to abide by. The pol-icy stated what action(s) management should take in situations as with the one with Jimmy and the 'other woman'. Management had every legal right to terminate both employees. In conclusion, the attorney told Jimmy, "you don't have a leg to stand on."

Action: Sam, since the interview has landed a well paying job. Her mother moved in with her to help with the kids, since the divorce with Jimmy became final. Jimmy has since then moved to a different city and started a new job. Surprisingly, support checks arrive on a monthly basis.

9

PRIVACY OF RECORDS
"Sara's Story"

Descriptive Analysis: Required records that include tax information, retirement plans, payroll, occupational illnesses, worker's compensation, are records almost all employers maintain on each employee. The above list of records is usually not the paper documentation that causes problem(s) for an employee. The following are examples of issues that can cause problems for an employee that usually show up as documentation in a personnel file:

• Why a promotion was not approved

• Why the employee was demoted

• Why the employee was fired

Most employers keep a 'paper trail' of everything that happens in the company. An example would be when a court case arises; the employer wants to have the correct paper documentation to prove his/her innocence.

Questions arise as to personnel files:

• Do you have the right to review your own file?

• Who else is allowed to see your file?

• What kind of information is being kept in the file besides what is legally required?

• What about medical records?

• If there are inconsistencies, do you have the right to insist that they are corrected by your employee, and in a timely manner?

Requesting permission to access your personal file may be allowed or rejected as to which state you reside. Many states will allow you to access your file. The review of your file is typically done in your own time and in the presence of a company official.

Again, there are exceptions to the rule. Employers may and can legally screen information from your records before you are able to review the file. This is usually directed as to the process of gathering pertinent information leading to a criminal investigation. If this is the case, then you are in real trouble!

It is always interesting to see what is in your employment file. These files are usually kept in a locked cabinet either in the Vice President's, Human Resource, or in the comptroller's office. The usual procedure to follow in order to gain access to your files is first, request permission from your supervisor, in some states this request is required in written form. Do not be surprised if you are not allowed to remove the file from whatever office it is being housed. Secondly, a company official may be present to make sure you do not alter any of the information or remove part of its contents. The feeling that is portrayed is one of total distrust.

The employment file includes the following: promotion, firing, disciplinary action, pay raise, termination, periodic evaluation, etc. In some states, medical records are treated differently from the general personnel file. Here are the rules that govern reviewing your personnel file:

- No one is allowed, except your employer to see your personnel file

- Any information in your file should be strictly job related

- Medical Records are treated differently. The *"Americans with Disabilities Act (ADA)* cover confidentiality of your medical records. According to this act, your medical information concerning your history or current condition must be kept on specific forms and kept separately from your personnel records.

The only personnel that can access the file are:

- Government official investigation as to the employer's compliance with the law

- Medical or First Aid personnel. This information is necessary if you have a condition that may require emergency treatment.

- If the individual has a disability that must receive special attention

- If theindividual's duties need to be restricted and a manager/supervisor needs to know

Interview: Sara's love for the fitness industry kept her from accepting a few higher paying positions in other fields. Her life-long attitude was, if you can't do what you truly love then life is not worth the trouble. Sara had an infectious laugh and every other comment would be followed with a fun-loving giggle. It was easy to see that this woman truly enjoyed life, although according to Sara that was not always the case.

Sara's eagerness to be part of a fitness business found her accepting a position she had performed fifteen years ago. She continued to say; "I did not care what job-level it was; all I wanted was the opportunity to workout (exercise) on a daily basis." To her, success was being involved in fitness and at the same time, earn enough money to pay the bills.

When the Athletic Director's position opened at an exclusive and well-established club, Sara applied immediately. During her interview she insanely promised to work twenty-four hours a day snd seven days a week. In her excitement as to the possibility of landing the job, she committed to activities that no rationale person could accomplish.

One of her responsibilities at the club was to be in charge of eleven personal trainers, which she added; the majority had been working at the club for the last ten years. Sara knew she had her work cut out for her; several of these personal trainers were set in their ways of doing things the way they wanted. The overall personal trainer's attitude was not always in the best interest of the club. In the past, this group had very little supervision. Sara admitted that usually when the inmates in the prison are given the keys to their cells and the run of the place, things typically go astray. In this case, with the former athletic directors allowing this group free reign, the monthly revenues did not reflect the true financial capabilities of the club.

Management now felt this group should be reorganized and retrained in the area of client-based, generated revenues. The question was how could Sara increase revenues and maintain the status quo of keeping harmony within this group. With a nervous giggle, she was the first to admit that she had no idea how to approach this closed knit group. This blasé' attitudinal group were not going to be happy campers when informed as to the mandate of the new company's policies. Sara knew that behavioral change was not going to be easy, and not going to happen over night.

Toiling for hours over a plan, she finally presented her ideas to upper management, who encouraged her to proceed with full support. Sara had enough previous experiences to realize that talk is cheap. She wondered how much management would really intervene if problems arose with this group.

The first step Sara attempted to have was a one-on-one conversation with each of the ten personal trainers. Thinking this would be a mechanism that would enable her to identify attitudes and expectations in concern with their jobs. It was an interesting experience, for nine out of the ten personal trainers merely sat through their individual times, coldly staring at her. Once again she started to giggle as she said "conducting interview sessions with this group was analogous to deer eyes in the headlights...nothing there." "You see in order to keep my sanity I had to find humor whenever I could." Regaining her composure, Sara explained that she knew the road ahead was going to be filled with opposition to any innovative revenue-generating idea she had.

Step number two was to have a staff meeting. Once again this turned out to be a total debacle. Although Sara decided not to be discouraged, she continued with her prepared agenda which included a proposed, but simple concept. In the past when the club was the only place to workout, members would walk through the door and be will-ing to stand in line in order to enlist the talents of the personal trainers. Most of the time, the trainers would be fully booked. Sara reminded everyone that business came to them; they did not have to make any type of effort to promote themselves and their talents. Now the market has changed, there is an abundance of competition. Fitness clubs are being erected all over the city, and the average individual has a plethora of choices ranging from location to monthly fees, programs, etc.

What Sara was suggesting was that each and everyone had to market themselves, an promote their talents on a daily basis. Being at the club during different hours would afford them exposure to different types of members. What the bottom line was simply each personal trainer would have to make an effort to enlist new clients.

According to Sara, you would have thought she just dropped the atom bomb. The look of horror on their faces was appalling. After a long silence, a young female trainer stood and announced that she had not gone to college for four years, and that she resented having to become a vacuum sweeper sales person. Sara promptly chimed in reminding the trainers that the more money the club made the more money they would make. She also reminded them that upper manage-ment wanted to increase revenues from the personal training program.

A few days passed by, thinking that everything was settled for it seemed that a few of the trainers were actually making an effort. It was not until Sara had to place a letter in her personnel file that she realized how the majority of the trainers really felt. In a manila envelope, marked personal was a gripe letter from four of the trainers complain-ing about Sara.

She admitted now that she can look back on the situation and laugh, but at the time, she felt like her insides were being pulled apart. How could they accuse her of the list of things ranging from not returning telephone calls immediately or being available at the club eighteen hours each day? Everything mentioned was ludicrous and friv-olous lacking any type of substance, but unfortunately, it was in her file. Sara thought if a new manager came on board and reviewed her personnel file, what would they think of her job performance. In addition, why was she not informed that these personal trainers had placed the letter in her file? Wasn't that sacred territory for only Sara's employer and her to see?

Remembering the meeting with her supervisor ensuring Sara that she would receive full support from management, she immediately requested a meeting. Sitting in her supervisor's office, Sara related the past events, reminding the supervisor that he endorsed her plan. Now the question was, is upper management going to do something about the personal trainer's coup?

The answer Sara received was not what she had wanted or expected. The supervisor told Sara that if the personal trainers were becoming upset, then it would be better not to upset the apple cart, but to just let things go as usual. Sara knew immediately, the personal trainers had met with the supervisor and probably gave an ultimatum that if they were not left alone, they would not only quit but also take their clients with them. Moreover, of course, the good ole boy system of weak management prevailed.

It was truly a catch-22, for without the trainer's efforts Sara would not accomplish the financial goals management insisted she achieve. Sara realized that she had dug her own grave with her initial enthusiasm when accepting the position. Sara laughed and said that this was the story of her life, jumping before looking. After seven months, Sara was recruited by another club, which offered higher pay and more managerial backing.

Action: Sara did take action with the unknowingly nasty letter that was placed in her personnel file. She wrote a retort, not justifying each attack, but stating what actually occurred. It seems the major writer (personal trainer) of the letter had wanted the athletic director's position and was angry and disappointed when the position went to Sara. The letter Sara wrote simply stated the above jealousy factor. If she had addressed each accusation, unsubstantiated as they were, it would have placed her on the same level as the accusers.

Recourse: The steps that Sara took were exactly perfect. Legal counsel was not necessary

10

INSTITUTIONAL DISCRIMINATION
"Kim Ye's Story"

Descriptive Analysis: There are different types of *discrimination* and *harassment*. Institutional discrimination constitutes a form of abuse that is repetitive to its victim(s). The injury of discriminatory denial of educational access through maintenance of a hostile environment can arise from a single or multiple acts of discrimination on the part of one or more individuals.

Most cases of *institutional discrimination* refer to professional advancement, but not always. The following is a list of some actions that may constitute this type of discrimination:

- Different standards of review (Kim Ye's case)

- Less recognition of achievement

- Lower salary increases

- Denial of benefits or promotions

- Denial of a fair grade

Attempting to prove *institutional discrimination* is extremely difficult. The individual must follow these steps:

1. Establish a *prima facie case of discrimination*. This is the easy part, all an individual has to do is demonstrate the person filing the charge is a qualified member of a *protected class* and was treated differently than his/her peers.

2. The individual filing the *charge* must explain the reason or reasons for seeking legal action.

3. The *burden of proof* then shifts back to the person being charged. In the academic world, this burden is rather impossible to meet mainly, because Many universities have definitive policies towards harassment and discrimination. Most reviews or decisions are

made behind closed doors in secrecy or by one controlling professor that has power over students.

Most universities have defintive policies towards harassment and discrimination. A person needs simply to refer to the institution's student handbook, a copy of which all individuals should receive as they enter the university.

Many universities have a two-paragraph explanation/disclaimer on the subject of *harassment* and *discrimination*. The following is an example:

"The University's aim is to provide a setting which is characterized by total respect for the individual student. This aim includes ongoing encouragement in order to develop his/her full potential. The University is pluralistic in nature and seeks to strive a setting that respects diversity of individuals and groups. This institution also promotes free exchange of information and ideas among staff, faculty, students, and guests.

The University is implicit in stating they will not tolerate any behavior, including physical or verbal conduct, which constitutes illegal discrimination or harassment in any form. The University is openly committed to helping victims of harassment and discrimination wherever they occur in the institution's community by taking corrective actions against violations of such policy. All individuals associated with the University's community are directly accountable for compliance with the policy. Note, violations may lead to disciplinary action which, in certain cases which deem severe, may result in immediate separation from the University."

Interview: Kim started the interview by expressing her love of learning and burning desire to earn a doctorate. She even had hopes, one day teaching in the university system while conducting research. With their only son soon to graduate from law school, and her husband Lee operating his own company, she thought the time had arrived. Even though she had wanted to attend the university where she received her master degree, Kim knew that would be impossible.

Fortunately, Lee being the sole owner of his company could decide on where it should be operated. Both Lee and Kim had always talked about moving to a warm climate. A few years previous, they both decided it would be a good time to relocate and move the company to Arizona. When Kim decided to return to school, there were very few options as to institutions of higher learning.

The last twenty years Kim had been associated with non-for profit organizations. Her major role was in the area of public relations. Kim enjoyed her involvement and found the job had wonderful benefits, extending from working with top-notch professionals to yearly bonuses. It was a tough decision to leave, but she felt relocating to a warm climate was well worth it.

Kim had the choice of applying at the local state university or drive 140 miles each way to attend a well-known private university. From previous experience, she knew the long commute would be difficult. While studying for her Masters degree, she drove 60 miles each way on a daily basis.

Telephoning the university was the start of a series of frustrating events. It should have been a sign of what was to come, but being the tenacious person she was, a few difficulties along the way were not going to stop her.

The first person she encountered was the professor in charge of Interdisciplinary Doctoral programs. Kim introduced herself to Dr. John Larson and proceeded to ask if he had time to answer a few questions in regard to the program. She continued by saying, she was not exactly sure of what course of action to pursue, for her background was in Public Relations. What happened next made Kim gasp for air. This professor Larson, under no uncertain terms responded by saying: "If you don't know what the hell you want then why are you wasting my time?" Kim trying to regain her composure replied, "I wish to pursue a degree, but am not quite sure what the university has to offer, and am merely asking for help." Dr. Larson then replied: "When you find out what you want out of life, call me back, but until then don't waste my time. He then slammed the phone down.

Kim thought ugly encounters with good ole boys only happened in the world of business. But now being rudely awakened and reminded after the telephone call, she realized if she wanted to pursue an advanced degree she would have to find someone willing to take the time to help her put a program together.

The next telephone call went to the department of Education. After explaining to the receptionist what she needed, the call was immediately directed to Dr. Loren Baker, acting chair of the Department. Kim still being upset from the previous call started by explaining what had happened in her conversation with Dr. Larson. She was surprised that Dr. Baker actually listened. Dr. Baker then reassured Kim that things are handled differently here in the department of Education. A meeting was arranged, a program planned, and Kim in 1996 started her graduate program specializing in the area of Business Education.

Everything seemed to be running smoothly when Kim met her major professor, Dr. Alex Cooperman. For the next three years or more, Dr. Cooperman would be in charge of assisting Kim with her program. Dr. Cooperman seemed amenable, but also at the same time wrapped up in his own research. To get an appointment with him was analogous to pulling teeth. He just was never available, and when he was seemed only to have time for his male students.

Kim believed that things started to go bad when she volunteered to be the coordinator of the International Educational Conference. This was a two-year commitment of pure organization; a strong asset Kim had lot's of experience. Her job was to organize presenters from all over the world. The gamut ranged from Australia to Malta, England to New Zealand. One hundred papers were selected for presentation at the conference. Nevertheless, the true essence of hosting the conference was to make Cooperman look good in front of his colleagues.

Cooperman knew she was the most qualified for the job, but had a disliking for Kim since their initial meeting. He felt and admitted openly at several different occasions that he felt Kim was good but did not like the idea that she was outspoken. That was the beginning of Cooperman's effort to impede Kim's doctoral program. He was smart enough not to touch the International Conference for he knew she could make him look good. However, at the same time he resented her to the max.

Two years of class work passed rather quickly. Kim's program was on automatic pilot, she knew what classes were required and in what semesters they would be offered. Kim admitted she was fortunate to have Lee's one hundred percent support. She also became friends with Maggie and Steve, two cohorts in the same program under the direction and control of the same major professor. Steve was the link Maggie and Kim used in order to understand where Dr. Cooperman was coming from and what he was thinking. Steve was great for he would on a daily basis keep Maggie and Kim abreast as to what was happening.

In the spring of the second year of study, Kim attended a national education conference. The theme was based on the concept of mentoring. The main speakers encouraged the audience to find a mentor (usually the major professor) and establish a business relationship of friendship and trust. The key speaker instilled in the audience the importance as to creating a life-long professional relationship with a current professional.

Returning to the university, Kim saw Dr. Cooperman walking down the hall. In her enthusiasm, she ran up to him and started sharing everything she had learned at the conference. Cooperman stopped her in the middle of a sentence and motioned her to come into his office and sit down. As Kim took a seat, Cooperman closed the door and positioned himself behind his dishevled desk. He then sat and stared at her with a cold gaze, after a few minutes he started to speak in his dry-boredom tone. He started by saying that if she expected him to be a mentor, not to count on it. Even though he was her major professor, his schedule kept him too busy. Then Kim wondered why he had time for all her male counterparts. What he was telling her in essence was that he could not really care less, end of conversation.

After a long talk with Lee, Kim decided since she was already admitted into candidacy (year after class work is completed, used strictly for gathering research for the completion of the dissertation) she would work around the clock to finish as soon as she could. Steve and Maggie suggested she contact three professors and ask them to be on her committee. The fourth member unfortunately had to be Cooperman. The main purpose of this group was to critique Kim's work, and offer her advice and guidance throughout her research. Kim taking everything at face value did not realize her committee was made up of two professors that were intimidated by Cooperman, and the third research specialist had so many doctoral students, he did not even have time for his family or himself.

Kim was required to submit research ideas to be approved by Dr. Cooperman. Every time she submitted a research proposal, he would turn her down. Finally, in almost total exasperation she countered him in his office, and asked him straight out, "What exactly do you want?" A creepy smile started to appear on his face, he then replied that he had an on-going study that he would highly suggest she consider for her dissertation. As he rose out of his chair, he handed Kim a proposal from another student and told her to read it.

Sequestering herself in the library for three hours, Kim re-read the proposal ten times. The area of study was of no interest to her and a topic that only would lead down a dead-end street. She could see herself conducting this research for the next year or two, in reality being Cooperman's indentured slave and gopher. Cooperman's intent was to coordinate as many of his doctoral students in which to collect and conduct research for his professional publications.

That night Kim related the story to Lee, who sat and listened intently. After what seemed to be a long time, Lee turned toward Kim and said: "I don't think you really have much choice but to do what Cooperman's requests." He then continued to say, "You don't have to put yourself through this, just walk away." She also knew she couldn't quit, for she had put too much time and effort into the program. Kim knew it would not give her an advantage; all she would be doing was cutting off her nose just to spite her face. The last thing she definitely did not want was to allow this egotistical, self-serving professor get the best of her.

Lee and Kim sat at the kitchen table until three o'clock in the morning laying out a plan. "OK, if Cooperman wants this work to be done, so be it." The next day, Cooperman wanted Kim to mail surveys out to over sixty experts around the world. Kim explained to Cooperman that this technique would take an incredible long amount of time. Instead of using the Post Office, Kim had the surveys over-nighted with pre-paid returns. This system cut the mailing time down to a tenth of what it would normally take to complete.

Steve over heard a telephone conversation Cooperman was having with one of his colleagues in which he expressed his surprise but along with it, his apprehension that Kim was moving too fast. It seems some academics have a problem when a student does not conform to what they feel is to be expected. A doctoral student should take a minimum of two years of required courses, pass the qualifying nine hour-exams, prove proficient in a statistical four-hour test, and then spend a year or more collecting data for a proposal and final defense. If a student has the ability to finish earlier than what the major professor is comfortable with, unfortunate consequences may occur, as seen in Kim's case.

Kim jumped through all the required hoops in less than a year's time. She worked diligently spending up to sixteen hours a day, seven days per week. While Kim was feverishly working, Cooperman received an opportunity to take a sabbatical (an approved one-year absence from campus). The approved leave was to go into effect in the spring of the next year.

A new dean of the College of Education was to take over in the next six months. It was common knowledge that Cooperman planned to get through as many of his doctoral students as possible, for this would prove to the new dean as to his effectiveness and worth to the university. Cooperman's schedule was packed full with appointments, ratio being five males students to one female student meeting. Maggie and Kim fought for times to have an audience with the major professor, but most of the time to no avail. They even tried to get a combination meeting with the two of them, providing lunch. It worked, but unfortunately, Kim needed more than one meeting to gain approval to proceed with her research.

Kim's proposal went smooth as silk. Her committee made suggestions as how to proceed and what they expected to see at the final defense. It was great, according to Kim to know what was to be expected. For a fleeting moment, she thought she had a team routing for her. The feeling of exhilaration did not last long, for Cooperman cornered her as she was leaving the room. With a smirk on his face, he turned towards Kim and gave a warning that her research better be more than excellent, for he realized that she was well liked by her committee. Even though they probably would not ask difficult questions in the final defense, he would come up with something that would "nail her to the wall. Taking a deep breath and maintaining her composure, Kim politely thanked Cooperman, and calmly walked out of the room.

Nine months into her year of candidacy, Kim had completed all the required work. The only thing left was to have Cooperman sign the last page on the graduate form giving her permission to present her research in the final defense. Months started to pass by; with Cooperman canceling each time the final defense was scheduled. Cooperman had a plethora of lame excuses, and unfortunately, Kim had no recourse. If she submitted a written complaint to the dean of the College of Education, Cooperman would make sure she never finished. It was a catch twenty-two no matter how one looked at it.

Ten months after Kim finished her dissertation, Cooperman finally signed off on the approval form. Even in the twelfth hour, he still had to prove his superior control by not signing the form until eleven fifty five pm, five minutes before the deadline. A doctoral candidate would have to wait another six months if the form was not signed and submitted on time.

The moment Cooperman signed the approval form, Kim looked him straight in the eyes and said: "It's been a real trip with you, till this day I don't know if it was worth it." On that note, she turned and walked away. Still to this day, Kim has never returned to the university.

As a sidebar, Kim was sitting in the kitchen of her home finishing lunch with Lee and her son. When she turned and asked the two of them, "Would you like to see me march in my graduation? or "Would you like to go see a movie?" Not to Kim's surprise, but the evening of the graduation, the Huang family enjoyed dinner followed by a movie.

Action: Kim had to decide how important it was for her to earn a doctorate. After considerable thought and discussion with her husband, the choice was made, and that was to do what ever was needed in order to complete the requirements.

Recourse: Kim had the option of filing a complaint with the university. If Kim elected to proceed with this action, she knew it was probable that she would never finish her doctorate, or if was allowed to finish, it would not be for many years.

Incidents of discrimination and harassment may be resolved through both formal and informal means. In certain situations, special assistance may be required in the selection of the best alternative to follow. Many universities have appointed intercessors available to staff, students, or faculty in cases of complaints or questions associated with discrimination and harassment. The intercessors are trained counselors who have an understanding of the importance of confidentiality, and will normally honor requests to take no future action. Although if an intercessor feels there may be some type of harmful threat, or a pattern of discriminatory/harassing behavior, this person has an obligation to take corrective action on behalf of the university represented.

There are other avenues of grievance procedures available to faculty, staff, and students. The intercessors main tasks are associated with providing assistance and confidentiality.

The responsibilities of the intercessors are:

1. Assists in facilitating informal resolution(s)

2. Consults if previous questions or complaints have not been resolved satisfactorily

3. Aids in the case of retaliation against the complainant

Formal procedures may also be used for resolution of complaints. Students that decide it is necessary to bring a formal complaint alleging illegal discrimination or harassment have numerous options depending on the identity of the alleged harasser. The following classifies possible harassers:

1. If the accused person is another student, the accuser should notify the judicial officer in the Dean's office. (if the university does not have this official, call the Dean's office and explain the situation). The judicial officer will determine if a charge is appropriate, if so, will convene with an administrative hearing. The individuals that make up this hearing are specially trained to hear complaints concerning discrimination and harassment.

2. If the accused person is on the university's staff, the accuser should address the complaint to the staff member's supervisor (department manager) who will follow the discipline and grievance procedures outlined in the University's Personnel Policies.

3. If the accused is a faculty member, the complaint will be forwarded to that faculty member's supervisor (department head) who will follow the grievance procedure outlined in the faculty handbook.

Institutions of higher learning have firm commitments to an environment that encourages, promotes, and protects free expression and inquiry. The discrimination and harassment policies are usually stated as not be intended to restrict freedom of speech or any legitimate form of artistic/visual expression.

Kim had a colleague that filed a complaint with the university. Her friend shared with Kim that she was extremely surprised as to how people around her treated her differently after the filing. Those who were not associated with the university were amazed that this type of discrimination actually took place, while those who worked at the university where in awe as to the thought that an individual could take legal action.

These individuals did not have a clue as to the price paid by someone proceeding with such charges.

Unfair treatment in academia is rampant, irrespective of the institutions and departments. For those individuals who work in the university system, academic harassment is to be dealt with.

Individuals that file justified claims of discrimination and harassment are many times perceived as troublemakers by the people involved in the case. It is a fine line to tread for once crossing over there is literally no turning back. Word travels fast around the academic community, and people that were once thought of as friends, no longer have any type of allegiance.

11

INEXPERIENCED MANAGEMENT
"Maggie's Story"

Descriptive Analysis: It is an interesting concept that if an individual aspires to practice medicine, a medical degree along with a two-year residency is required. If the individual has a desire to practice law, then an extremely difficult examination has to be successfully passed. In operating a company one would think there would also be a list of requirements, but there are no required proficiency tests that have to be passed, no college degree earned, or even relevant, hands-on experience required.

Directing and operating a business that produces profits, as anyone would admit, can be challenging. Qualified or not, anyone is allowed to try as long as they have the financial means. It is analogous to being American and having certain rights. Even if the individual is young, stupid and foolish, they are allowed a chance. There are no laws stating what the qualifications are to head and operate a company.

Many inexperienced managers try to mask their lack of experience and know how by pretending they are adults. The sad thing concerning this scenario is that these "wet behind the ears fledglings" can ruin a senior professional's career.

Interview: Maggie was currently teaching as an adjunct at a local university. In the mean time hoping a full-time position would open so that she could be fully employed with a paycheck to match. Even though her husband kept reminding her that she did not have to work, she wanted to contribute.

At the end of the second semester, she approached the head of the department and inquired as to possibilities of teaching positions opening? The chair head cordially smiled and flatly said "No." Every position in this department is concretely shut; in order to qualify you may have to wait for someone tenured to die. "All right" Maggie replied, "If that's where it's at, then it may be time for to check out other possibilities."

A few days later while playing a tennis match, one of her friends told her about a computer sales position that was available. Evidently, the current sales employee decided to marry and move to Mobile, Alabama. Great Maggie thought, I might as well go for it, hoping all along that they weren't looking to replace the position with a twenty five year old computer geek. Maggie was fortunate in that she did not look her age of forty-two. By staying in excellent shape and having good genes, she had a youthful appearance of possibly being in her mid-thirties.

After dinner that evening, Maggie decided it was time to have a talk with Dave. He completely surprised her by sitting and tentatively listening to her idea. His only comment was, "I like your initiative and am pleased you are thinking of getting back into the industry, but be cautious. I am vaguely familiar with the company and recall that most of the employees are young males. Your educational qualifications may appear intimidating to them, which could cause problems in the end." What Dave was saying was correct, even though Maggie did not wear her degrees on her sleeve for everyone to see, she did have to consider the possibility of jealously.

Maggie decided after carefully thinking through all ramifications, nothing ventured nothing gained. She still wanted to apply. Maggie requested an interview and prepared herself thoroughly as to what questions she may have to answer. The first interview went smoothly, after an hour, Maggie felt relieved that the questions were easy to answer and that the interviewer seemed quite pleased. Thinking she had the job, Maggie was shocked when the interviewer telephoned her and asked to meet with her for a second interview. Quickly obliging, Maggie agreed to return to the company later that afternoon.

The second interview went well, but still no offer. After three interviews, lasting an hour per session, financial terms were finally verbally agreed. Maggie accepted the position and inquired as to the starting date. Hoping it would be at the beginning of the next month, for Dave and the kids had planned a trip to Europe for ten days before the school year started.

The next day when Maggie arrived to sign the contracts, the first thing she noticed was the financial terms were considerably altered. After considering everything involved, she decided to confront the interviewer. Maggie explained, in reviewing the final paper work she found the terms originally agreed upon quite different. She continued to explain that the terms were unacceptable, and at this time would not be in a position to accept the job.

The interviewer stared at Maggie for a moment, then apologized and handed the paper work to the secretary with instructions to alter the agreement. He then turned back to Maggie and asked if she could wait a few minutes for the changes to be made. Maggie agreed to wait and complete all the employment forms. Walking out of the office, she felt a sense of relief.

The first three months were difficult but rewarding. Maggie seemed to be settling in rather nicely. One of her major responsibilities was the coordination of five major accounts. These corporations already had purchased the primary software. All Maggie had to do was to make sure the software was being used effectively.

Unfortunately in January, Maggie's supervisor became ill and resigned. A month later, the company hired a replacement. Maggie had an uneasy feeling the new supervisor would be trouble just by the expression on his face when she met him the first day.

Around early afternoon the new supervisor strutted into Maggie's office and without saying a word sat down in the only chair, folded his arms, and said: "well, who are you and tell me something about your background." Maggie realized by the arrogance being exhibited, she needed to tread water and proceed slowly and carefully in how she presented herself. He then requested Maggie to describe her job description and what she did in a typical day. All the while she was talking, Maggie kept wondering as to the age of this new supervisor and how much experience he actually had in the industry. Looking at him, Maggie surmised that he was in his late twenties and by his stiff-rigid demeanor could only guess how much experience he possessed. Maggie had always prided herself in judging human characteristics, and what she saw in front of her worried her. This guy appeared nervous, unsure of himself and intimidated by older and more experienced/educated people. Unfortunately, Maggie knew the warning signs.

Using a soft but polite tone, Maggie asked the new supervisor what his background encompassed. Now thinking back it probably was not the best thing to do at the time. Realizing this, she quickly blurted out that she did not mean any disrespect, but wasn't sure if the new supervisor realized that?"

With a scornful look on his face, he bluntly answered the question with: "I have been an entrepreneur for the last ten years." From being around Dave (CEO of a large publicly traded firm) she knew that when someone came up with that type of answer, he had not been doing much of anything in the last couple of years.

At dinner that night, Maggie elaborated on the events of the day saving the meeting with the new supervisor for last. After a complete rundown of the situation, Dave looked at her and said that things will probably change, and unfortunately not for the good. Dealing with inexperienced, non-professionals will quickly become extremely frustrating. In addition, from what you have been telling me, his reorganization plans only include promoting the young, male employees at the company. Dave was right, not one female had been promoted. Maggie's husband continued to say, "You know Maggie, that's the first sign the good ole boy system will probably prevail." He added, "I'm not sure how long you will be able to tolerate this type of work environment."

Two weeks after the new supervisor arrived, he requested each department to submit an inclusive report of daily events. Maggie responded immediately by detailing her relationship with each one of her accounts. Two hours after she submitted her report, she received a call from the supervisor's secretary requesting her immediate presence in his office. Thinking there was nothing out of the ordinary, she dropped everything she was doing and reported to his office. After knocking on the door, Maggie heard a voice: "Come in." As she entered the office, she could feel the tension in the air. "What do you think you are doing here submitting this type of report? These are not your accounts. I heard from other employees you were given the responsibilities to merely monitor their software applicatons. You did not bring these accounts into the company. As a matter of record, I only see two accounts that you enlisted."

Maggie felt the hair on the back of her neck stand up and a clammy feeling spread over her body. Her first response was, yes, someone else brought the accounts in, but I am the one that is maintaining their loyalties to this company. And further more, I have only been here a short while, it takes time to cultivate new clients. The new supervisor rigidly sat and stared at Maggie. At that point, she knew there really wasn't anymore to say. Standing up, she turned and left the office.

As she walked out of the company's front door, she glanced back at the receptionist's desk to see two of the young, male employees looking at her and laughing as they gave each other the high-five sign. Maggie explained that she had a difficult time trying to comprehend what was happening. She never caused any trouble and felt she performed her responsibilities as a professional. Still to this day, Maggie can't remember how she got home, for to her it all seemed a blur.

The next day when she reported to work, the first thing to arrive at her desk was a memo informing her that she no longer was in charge of her assigned accounts. If she wanted to stay with the company, she would have to bring in her own clients.

Shortly after, Maggie resigned. Talking with Dave one night the conversation turned toward what happened at the company. When the inexperienced young manager came on board, he was obviously intimidated by anyone with professional expertise. Not wanting to be out done, his first self-directed task was to get rid of anyone that could possibly stand in his way. Maggie heard from one of her colleagues that her replacement was a young male right out of college.

Three months after Maggie left, the supervisor faced a variety of problems that he was unable to handle. The problems escalated to the point where he would arrive at the company early in the morning, hide behind closed doors in his office during the day, and after hours when most of the employees were gone, sneak out of the back door. Shortly after, he was fired.

Action: Maggie knew and resented being burned by a young, inexperienced supervisor. All she could do was to complain to the company's CEO and hope for the best. She explained in her exit interview, the young supervisor's problem was a lack of experience and people skills needed to operate a growing tech-company. It was common knowledge as to the numerous complaints from old and new accounts in concern with the supervisor's unprofessional management.

When Maggie walked out of the exit interview, she knew nothing was going to happen. However, she reminded herself as she walked away, it may not happen now, but his inexperience will catch up with him, and it did.

Recourse: Maggie could have elected to file charges of harassment with the EEOC. The disparate treatment she experienced would have backed her claim. According to the law, no individual should ever be demeaned the way she was in the workplace.

12

INOPPORTUNE TIMING
"Georgia's Story"

Descriptive Analysis: The possibility of being fired, dismissed, or laid off is a fear of most workers. The professional workplace is highly competitive. An individual must stay keenly astute to the relationships between workers and management. Company policy must be understood and adhered to for the overall benefit of the company.

When the individual is the "new kid on the block", it is important to learn early in the game what constitutes the corporate pecking order. Attending the first staff meeting, an individual should be able to identify certain clues as to the dynamics of who the "movers and shakers" are in the company. Sitting, listening, and watching, an individual will most likely be able to identify the structure of the hierarchy.

In almost every company, there are certain "sacred cows." People with this status either are the favorites of upper management, or have some stipulation in their contractual agreement. These people should never be placed in an uncompromising situation(s), otherwise be ready to pay the price.

Interview: Not all the situations in this book have a positive nature. In Georgia's case, she did not follow the protocol of the company, and therefore suffered the consequences of justified dismissal. Here is Georgia's story.

A woman with bright red short hair and brilliant blue eyes sat across from me one afternoon and related the following experience. Georgia started the interview by saying; she now realizes that the blame cannot be directed soley at upper management. She was the first to admit that she was guilty for the fax-paux that happened.

Georgia explained, she always worked for a large firm ever since graduation from college. As the years passed by, in order to advance her career, she thought it would be advantageous to earn a Masters of Business degree (MBA). A few of her co-workers had recently enrolled in an "Executive Master of Business Administration degree program"

(EMBA). To qualify for the program, an individual needed the following:

1. Earn an undergraduate degree from a reputable institution

2. Five years management experience

3. Score a minimum of a 1000 (score) on the Graduate Record examination (GRE)

Georgia with a sparkle in her eyes quickly added, "The best part about the program was the company would pay the tuition." Georgia's only concern was the short amount of time she had been employed with this particular company. Six months of employment still classified her as a new employee. She thought there may be a policy stating an employee before receiving tuition re-imbursement, may have to be with the company at least a year.

With an EMBA, compared to a MBA, the tuition is usually doubled. The university views EMBA students as being older, professional, and fully employed in a managerial position. This type of program is usually encouraged by most companies resulting in the payment of the total tuition. The program is designed for students to bring to the table a variety of actual workplace experiences. It is a different mindset than what exists in the regular MBA program, where many of the students have not had the workplace experiences.

The first thing Georgia had to request was to get the company's approval for the two-year course. The classes would be held every Saturday, from eight in the morning to four thirty in the afternoon. These types of class times would not interfere with her weekly work schedule. Her supervisor informed Georgia, all she had to do was to fill out a massive amount of paper work for the Human Resource Department. Surprisingly, approval came within two days.

The major problem that Georgia un-knowingly encountered was that as she progressed through the program, the more knowledge she acquired the more dangerous she became. At the time, she did not realize that knowledge is power, and no one told her it was a fine-line to travel. Georgia admitted that she now realizes the importance of knowing when to use this power, and when not to use this power. She continued to say; the program opened her eyes to many things that in the past she accepted as the norm.

The semesters passed by quickly, with subjects such as Accounting, Finance, Business Law, Operations, etc. Meanwhile, Georgia's work with the company was progressing without a hitch. Her direct reports, consisting of twenty employees were producing at the expected rate. Everything seemed quite copasetic until the day arrived for the divisional board meeting. It was mandatory for all managers to present a thirty-minute overview of their department's quarterly financials.

The meeting was well into the third hour when a young male manager presented. Georgia admitted, "I had not slept well the night before, and was having a difficult time keeping my eyes open." Since she had already presented, Georgia could sit back and relax. About half way through the young manager's presentation, Georgia in a very sleepy mode glanced at the power point presentation. She could not believe her eyes, the financial figures the young man was presenting, were all wrong. Georgia knew if he got away with this, it would make the rest of the group look bad. "How could he stand up there in front of everyone, and lie?" Instead of sitting quietly and thinking through what she was going to say, Georgia blatantly blurted out that he fabricated his presentation. The numbers, according to her did not truly reflect his department's earnings for that quarter.

Georgia then admitted sheepishly, it was not the right thing to do or the right time to do it. Every one seated at the long oval desk, turned and glared at her. She then realized that she was in a difficult position, one that would be almost impossible to escape. Not only had she betrayed a colleague, but also she stepped on the toes of one of the most popular up and coming managers at the company. In other words, he was also one of the golden boys on his way up the corporate ladder. All Georgia could think of was, "Oh God, I really blew it this time."

Georgia started talking at a rapid pace. She suddenly stopped and said: "Wow, I am getting all worked up in this interview, the same way I did in the board meeting." She said she did not know what got into her, instead of sitting back and keeping her mouth shut, she started nervously rambling on about what ever came to mind. Georgia knew it was common, unspoken knowledge that co-workers stick together. If you have a criticism of a supervisor or colleague, you confront the person face to face, behind close doors, but never if front of others, especially upper management. There was no way to save face, for either Georgia, or especially the manger doing the presentation.

Georgia apologized profusely, but to no avail, the damage had been done. Her colleagues all became anxiously silent, most of them seen staring at the floor. This was the cue for Georgia to get up, quickly and quietly leave the room. As soon as she returned to her office, she picked up her brief case and left for home. That night Aaron, her live-in boy friend, was on a business trip in San Francisco. Georgia admitted, she was relieved Aaron was not there. The last thing she wanted was to have to muster up enough energy to re-live the events of the day. All Georgia wanted was a piece of solitude. Before going to bed, she opened a bottle of wine, and after finishing the last drop, fell into a deep sleep.

The next morning when the alarm clock started sputtering, Georgia said it sounded like a jackhammer in her head. What a hangover. The alarm clock was bad enough, but then the telephone starting ringing, that was the last straw.

Georgia admitted, "I sat and stared at the phone for what seemed like an eternity. Not wanting to pick up the phone was a justified fear, since what had occurred the day before. How could she have done such a stupid thing? There she sat staring at the phone, when all of a sudden in a weak moment, Georgia picked up the receiver and hoarsely said "hello." Thank heavens it was only Aaron calling to see if she was all right. He admitted, she gave him quite a fright. Aaron in his typical scolding manner, said, "I called ten times last night without an answer. At one point, I was tempted to call the police and have them check on you."

Aaron was right; Georgia should not have finished off a bottle of wine, especially on an empty stomach. About thirty seconds of silence passed, Georgia started crying like a baby while at the same time, attempting to explain what had happened the day before. After pouring out her guts, Georgia said there was an uncomfortable long pause. She knew when she heard Aaron clear his voice; he was deep in thought, trying to assimilate the facts. Aaron finally commented by saying, "Georgia, I feel bad for you, I know how much the job means to you." In a pragmatic tone, Aaron continued to say that sometimes things happen for the best. "I know that is not truly consoling at this time. Just be ready for the consequences, for situations like this usually do not have pretty endings."

With her head still spinning, Georgia said in a desperate tone, "I'm going to call in sick today, I just can't go in." Like a schoolhouse teacher reprimanding a student, Aaron told Georgia that would not be a wise decision. He told her, calling in sick would be the worst thing to do, especially after yesterday. Even though the hangover was bad, she had to get into the shower, drink a gallon of black coffee and go into the office. "Georgia", Aaron said in a strong positive manner, "You have to accept the consequences, no matter what ever they may be. "Now listen, you need to pull yourself together." Sit down at the kitchen table and write down on a piece of paper, exactly what you expect to happen when you walk in the office this morning. Now, think it through, what can be the worst-case scenario? How will you act if some heavy questions are shot your way? Be prepared with a plan before entering the office."

It sounded so easy when Aaron explained what to do, "yea easy for him because he didn't have to face his accusers. Georgia paused,

"Aaron, I really am not sure if I can do this or not." "Well" Aaron replied, "You have no choice."

At eight-thirty, Georgia arrived at the office. Not being surprised to see a note on her desk, requesting her immediate presence in the main conference room. When she walked in, she immediately noticed, three people. The young manager whom she derided the day before, a Human Resource representative and her direct report.

Barbara (Georgia's supervisor) started the meeting by saying that it was unfortunate what had happened the day before, but the clock cannot be turned back. She continued pontificating in her usual manner, reminding everyone present, the whole concept of the their business was "unified thinking." In other words, everyone works together for the good of the company. "Yesterday Georgia, you attacked a colleague unmercifully in front of everyone. This type of behavior destroys co-worker relationships within the internal structure of the company." Barbara then sat back in her big leather chair, took off her glasses, and started nervously bridging her hands. Georgia recognized the visual cues and knowing what she was up against, the only thing she could do, was resign.

Georgia stood up and looked directly at the young manager, "Listen, you know your numbers were incorrect, everyone could see that." Then lowering her voice a few octaves, she calmly said, "You screwed up, I brought it to the attention of others thinking they would back me, but they didn't. Turning toward Barbara, Georgia acknowledged the need for all employees to work in a communal mode, and then she formally apologized for yesterday's outburst. "Evidently I'm not the team player I thought I was." With her head held high, she turned and walked out of the conference room.

The next day, Georgia met with Barbara and discussed the possibility of a *severance package*. Aaron was the one who strongly suggested Georgia ask. She was pleasantly surprised when Barbara agreed to two months full pay along with extended insurance coverage. If it had not been for Aaron's insistence, she would have left with nothing.

Today Georgia operates her own consulting agency. Laughingly she said, "I love being independent, and able to choose whom I want to work with." She said, "I could never return to corporate America and play the game,"

Action: Georgia was fortunate; she had the financial capability to start her own consulting company. She admitted as to the difficulty in getting an independent business started. Clients do not usually appear over night, and there has to be some type of monetary assets to keep afloat.

Georgia was also smart in starting her own company and working for herself. It did not require reworking her resume' and going through extensive explanations as to the reason she left her last position. Her only regret in separating from the company was the fact; she now had to pay her own tuition. Georgia freely admitted, "The first thing I had to do, was prioritize my spending. In an upbeat tone, she said the decision was easy. All her adult life, she had wanted her own company, therefore the money she had saved over the years, went towards developing her dream. Georgia's closing thought was, "Maybe someday I will finish my EMBA, but not now."

Recourse: Employers have traditionally had freedom to hire and fire in the workplace, although a number of recent laws and legal rulings restrict these rights. As a result, individuals who have been laid off or fired have power to negotiate severance pay and any other benefits. In return, these individuals have to waive any rights to sue based on a claim of discrimination or wrongful discharge.

Unless an individual has a written employment contract for a stated number of years, the person can be fired. Here are a few examples:

1. Violating company rules (Georgia's case)

2. Incompetence

3. Sleeping or taking drugs on the job

4. Company down sizing due to a decrease in revenues

5. Merger with another company (just to mention a few)

In most cases, employers are not required to provide any notice before releasing an employee from his/her job. Although, an employer must deal with the individual on a fair and honest basis.

If the individual elects not to challenge the legality of the dismissal, it is crucial to document the circumstances. An example would be if the individual applies for unemployment insurance benefits and the former employer refuses to approve the application, the individual would need to prove the reason(s) for the dismissal, were not related to misconduct type of behavior(s).

Legally there was nothing for Georgia to pursue. She made a major mistake and paid for it by losing her job. There is no court in the world that would defend her actions.

13

SEXUAL HARASSMENT
"Martha's Story"

Descriptive Analysis: *Sexual harassment* is prevalent in workplaces across the United States. This type of *harassment* still poses to be a daily problem, especially for women. According to legal terms, *sexual harassment* is any unwelcome sexual conduct in the workplace that creates an intimidating, hostile, and offensive working environment. To define the harassment term even further, sexually harassing behavior encompasses offensive belittling jokes/remarks, full-fledged pornography, and outright sexual assault. The degree of each category is not important, but what is relevant, is that an individual is experiencing unsolicited and unwelcome treatment.

Definition: *Sexual Harassment* is a form of sexual discrimination that violates *Title VII of the Civil Rights Act of 1964.* The *EEOC* has definable guidelines that reference two types of harassment:

1.   *Hostile environment*

2.   *Quid pro quo*

Hostile Environment: *Sexual harassment* conduct that interferes with an individual's work performance or creates an intimidating, offensive workplace environment. This definition implicitly includes sexual advances, requests for sexual favors, and physical/verbal conduct that connotes a sexual nature.

Quid Pro Quo: Requests for sexual favors, unwelcome sexual advances, and other physical/verbal implication(s) promote this type of *sexual harassment.* Submission or rejection of sexual conduct by an individual is used as the basis for managerial-employment decisions directly or indirectly affecting the individual. Also included as part of this definition is: conduct made explicitly or implicitly as a condition of an individual's employment contract.

- *Unwelcome Sexual Conduct*: The individual regards the conduct as offensive or undesirable. The conduct is classified as sexually unwelcome in reference to the individual not inciting or soliciting it.

- *Victim:* The victim in a sexual harassment case may be either female or male. In addition, the victim does not have to be the individual harassed, but one that is affected by the offensive nature of the conduct.

- *Harasser:* This individual may be either a woman or a man. The title of harasser may be associated with: (1) supervisor, (2) agent of the employer, (3) supervisor in another department, or a (4) co-worker.

EEOC 's Determination: If the *EEOC* is presented with conflicting evidence as to whether the sexual advancements were welcomed or not, the commission will examine the record as to the total picture. The Commission will review and evaluate each situation on a case-by-case basis. The investigators look for a determination as to the consistency or inconsistently of the victim's conduct, in reference to the assertion that the sexual conduct was considered 'unwelcome'.

Interview: Martha was excited that she finally had the chance to return to the professional world of advertising. After twenty years of raising a family and supporting her husband's career, she was more than ready.

Martha started the interview by stating that she felt she was simply a "plain Jane." Although she realized at a young age that she was not physically attractive, she did feel strongly that her strengths were in having a creative and intuitive mind.

High school and the dances proved to be uneventful, almost depressing. Around the age of twenty, Martha had reached a new low level of self-esteem where she just knew her physical appearance would not attract anyone from the opposite sex. Then one day, Joe arrived and swept her madly off her feet. That was twenty-years ago, and not a day goes by that he does not tell Martha how beautiful and important she is to him. Joe turned out to be a good husband and her best friend. Sex after twenty years to either of them was not that important, but being friends and having someone to talk with at the end of the day was all that mattered.

Martha accepted a position with a small advertising agency. She thought this would be a comfortable re-entry back into the field. The first day at the office she was formally introduced to the staff of five which included: a young male in the accounting department around twenty-five, two women secretaries in their forties, a female office manager in her late thirties, and last but not least, an unattractive salesman in his late fifties. Well, that was the group according to Martha.

The first day of work proved to be rather uneventful. The day proceeded along a format of becoming accustomed to the workplace environment. The office manager told her to take her time and familiarize herself with each person's responsibilities.

Martha's office cubicle was located next to Matt, the fifty-year-old salesman. With thin walls separating the two offices, she could clearly hear every conversation Matt had. "You see" Martha replied, "all he did all day was to sit on the phone and shoot the bull handing out one story after another.

Moving into the second week of work, everything seemed to be going quite nicely, except for Matt (the salesman) constantly going out of his way to engage Martha in trivial conversations. At first, Martha thought it was nice to have such a friend, but then realized that Matt's agenda was quite different from hers.

About the middle of the third week, Matt started sending flowers along with cards telling her what a great job she was doing. Next were the unexpected meetings in the company staff room. Whenever Martha went to take a break, there was Matt.

He knew through casual conversation with Martha that Joe traveled a lot, and was out of town most of the week. After being with the company for six weeks the telephone calls started. Each night around ten o'clock, the phone would ring. "Hi…how are you doing? Are you all cleaned up and ready for bed? I know you are all alone, would you like some company?" This went on night after night. Martha was embarrassed to tell Joe when he returned home on Friday nights. She found herself in a dilemma without knowing where to turn.

At first, the attention Matt was giving her was exciting, although she would not admit that to anyone. However, after awhile the attention became exceedingly bothersome. On one hand, she was flattered that he looked twice at her for not many men (according to her) found her attractive, but then look what it was doing to her job performance. She found that she was having a difficult time concentrating for Matt was continuously peeking over the wall to see what she was doing.

Matt's interruptions became a regular occurrence. She wondered if she should report him to the office manager, but then decided against the idea. One day he entered her office unannounced. Being on the telephone, she motioned him to come in and sit down. That was the first mistake of the day for Matt sat and waited patiently for Martha to finish her business call. When she hung up the phone, he stood up and walked over to her. "Martha, you sounded upset last night when I called. I realize being alone is not easy, and I would have been more than happy to come over and comfort you, even if it took all night." He then reached over and patted her on the thigh, then winked, and exited the office.

What was she to do? She had never been in this position before. Matt's outward advancements were becoming more blatant by the day. She did not want to complain to her manager for she was the new kid on the block and was in the process of proving her value to the company. How would it sound if she approached her manager and started complaining about a co-worker? She decided to toughen it out and circumvent him whenever she saw him approaching. This plan was not as easy as it sounded. Matt was a triple-A personality and was not one to take no for an answer.

Two more months passed, and Martha found herself obsessed with thinking of ways of how to stay away from Matt. This reached a point where the quality of her job performance started to slip, and unfortunately the time her supervisor requested her presence in her office for a six-month review. The first thing out of her manager's mouth was that she did not understand how and why Martha started out great, but as time passed, the quality of her work seemed to diminish. She looked Martha straight in the eyes and asked for an explanation.

Martha's mind started racing a million miles a minute. Should she tell her of the problem she was experiencing with Matt? Alternatively, should she just explain that she was having a problem at home? Martha explained that it was a tough decision to make, for she did not want to be classified as a complainer, but at the same time, she knew she needed help. She then sighed and said, "I made a major mistake; I lied to you about the situation in the office." The supervisor seemed to accept the explanation and in closing offered Martha a few encouraging words.

Three weeks later Martha was pulling her hair out and ready to scream. At this point, she could no longer take any more of his sexual advances, as subtle as they may have seemed. Friday night when Joe returned home she sat down, mingled with tears, related the past events at the office. She was not a bit surprised that Joe sat silently, thinking, and pondering over what to do. Being married to him for twenty years, she had a great insight to his demeanor. After what seemed an eternity, Joe finally responded. "Martha, I don't see any alternatives except start looking for another job." Martha once again could feel the tears well-up in her eyes…"Joe this is the first real job in a long time…and I truly am enjoying the work except for the situations that occur with this salesman." Then Martha said: "no, I am not going to quit and be run out by this low life individual. He is not going to get the best of me and cause problems in my life."

Joe had seen this look on Martha's face only twice in their marriage. He knew once she made up her mind there was no changing it. "Ok, what's your plan?" Martha confessed that she did not know very much about the law, but knew she had rights, at least when it came to sexual discrimination. She stated that she was not going to let this guy get away with such inappropriate behavior, especially at her expense.

The challenge was to find an attorney. Joe came through with a name of an attorney he had met at a seminar about a year ago. Martha took the number and called for an appointment. Sitting in the attorney's office, Martha started to second-guess her motives and wondered if she should just get up and leave. It was too late, for the attorney was entering the room. Fred Cunningham was purported to be one of the top discrimination attorneys in Seattle. Martha kept her fingers crossed that he was not going to charge her a steep fee for his services.

Fred sat and silently listened to Martha's story. At times, he would nod in agreement to what she was saying. After she finished, he took a deep breath and turned to face her directly. "Martha, I have to tell you up front that this is going to be a tough case, the U.S. Court of Appeals recently reversed a decision for sexual harassment. It seems that the evidence the woman presented in the case was very similar to hers. Fred quickly added that he did not mean they would lose, but wanted to forewarn Martha as to what she might be up against. He continued to say that he agreed that the salesman's behavior was in appropriate and realized the hardship she experienced.

Martha becoming impatient and wanted to know why did the Appeals Court reverse the decision? Fred said he had a copy of the proceedings and started to dig through his drawer of discrimination files. Not having any luck locating the document, in an exasperated tone, he shouted to his assistant. "Sherrie, can you come in here please." With a smile on her face, Sherrie appeared at the door holding a manila file in her hands. Is this what you need Counselor? Fred looking sheepishly said: "What took you so long" then he winked at Martha and laughingly said, "don't know what in heaven's name I would do without her?" Sherrie evidently had over heard the conversation and thought she would help by finding the information needed.

After Fred thanked Sherrie she turned an exited the office, looking over at Martha with a gleam in her eyes. "Ok, here it goes the results of the reversal." The court felt for behavior to constitute sexual harassment it had to be pervasive and severe, and nothing proved to be of that degree in the case.

In Martha's case, having Matt the salesman tell her she looked nice, and sending her flowers would not fit the bill. Also calling her at night just showed caring and did not allude to abnormal behavior.

The women in the reversed case accused her harasser of the following:

1. Accused the harasser of putting his hand on her right thigh during a conversation held in her office.

2. Accused the harasser of lifting the hem of her dress a few inches...while asking what kind of material it was?

3. Accused the harasser of saying demeaning things...like he knew she did not have much experience, and that women are like meat, and that men need variety in women...

4. Accused the harasser of telephoning late at night and asking questions as to what the woman was wearing or if she was already in bed?

   - The court stated that telling someone he or she is beautiful is not exactly a sexual comment, and if it were, a reasonable person would not find it offensive. Flirtation is not sexual harassment.

   - In regard to the telephone calls, neither the content nor the frequency suggested obsessive or stalker-like behavior.

   - Asking someone if they are in bed when calling late at night is what the court classified as 'common courtesy' and does not necessarily have an importer sexual connotation.

In conclusion, the court ruling alleged harassment in this case exemplifies 'ordinary tribulations of the workplace'.

Martha then asked how the EEOC would view her case. Fred said they would first evaluate the totality of the situation(s) to ascertain the (1) nature, (2) frequency, (3) context, and (4) directive of the intended remarks. He continued to say that important factors may include whether the remarks were of a hostile or a derogatory nature, or whether the alleged harasser singled out the charging party, and last but not least, the type of relationship between the charging party and the alleged harasser.

"In some cases a single incident can and may constitute sexual harassment. In 'quid pro quo' cases, a single sexual advance may be classified as harassment if it is associated with the denial or granting of employment or employment benefits. Now, there is something called a "hostile environment claim" which usually requires identifying a pattern(s) of offensive conduct. Even one single, severe incident of harassment may be sufficient to constitute a Title VII violation. And in your case Martha, it was ongoing occurrences that happened over a significant amount of time."

Fred then advised Martha to take time and think things over. Considering the information Fred offered, Martha needed to ask herself if she still felt she had a solid case. Fred continued saying that it was unfortunate for this reversal to come out at this time; for it did not help Martha's case.

Martha returned home and immediately explained to Joe what the outcome was of the meeting with the attorney. A week later, she called Fred to inform him that she was not going to proceed with the charge. She had discussed it with her husband and they came to the decision to quit the job, find a new place of employment and go on with life. Now in her life she was not willing to spend the time fully engaged in a legal fight, spend money on fees, when the timing and the merits of the case were not the most advantageous.

Action: What action or actions could Martha have pursued? The first thing she needed to do was to approach Matt, and inform him that his conduct was not welcomed and that it must stop. This step is important for the victim to communicate that the conduct is unwelcome, especially when the alleged harasser may have some reason to believe that the advance(s) may be indeed, welcomed. If confronting the harasser face to face proves to be too difficult, then Martha's own conduct should demonstrate that Matt's (harasser) advances are unwelcome. Martha needed to use any employer complaint mechanism or grievance system available. If all failed, she then should have notified the EEOC immediately.

In the above case, Martha may have elected to continue to pursue legal action. If she was disappointed with the counsel's advice as to the merit(s) of her case, she had full right to contact another attorney for a second opinion.

Recourse: There are laws that protect individuals from sexual harassment. *The Equal Employment Opportunities Commission* (1980) issued regulations defining this type of harassment. The Commission stated that this form of discrimination, upheld by the *Civil Rights Act 1964*, is held to be illegal.

If the *harasser* ignores the victim's oral requests to stop, then the victim should write a letter demanding an end to the behavior. If the *harasser* continues, copy his/her supervisor with the demand letter. Then, if the supervisor is sympathetic with the *harasser*, send the demand letter with a cover letter to his/her boss. In other words, keep on going up the company ladder until someone takes serious notice.

It is also important to keep a detailed paper trail (journal) of the specifics as they relate to any of the situations. Include the date, time, witnesses, and brief synopsis of the situation. Be specific as to how this type of treatment is affecting the job performance. If the employer has given the individual high marks in periodic reviews, copies should be immediately made and kept in the personnel file. This type of documentation is helpful in the case where the employer retaliates by attempting to transfer or fire the employee simply by giving the employee a poor job performance rating.

Legally, under the federal Civil Rights Act or under a state fair employment practices statute, an individual can file a civil lawsuit for damages. Before filing the lawsuit, the employee is first required to file a claim with a government agency. To make this point clearer, an individual pursuing a claim under the *Civil Rights Act* must first file a claim with the federal *Equal Employment Opportunity Commission (EEOC)*, and a similar format is required under some state laws. Remember that laws differ from state to state. Be sure to find out what laws are applicable in the state of residency.

The filing agency will issue a document referred to as a *"right to sue" letter*. This letter allows the individual to take the case to court. When filing an action for *sexual harassmen*t, the majority of individuals need legal counsel.

Recently two Federal Court Rulings (6-28-98) were determined and based on the two cases presented the following:

Case 1: June 1998—Burlington Industries, Inc. v. Ellerth: A woman resigned from her job after a supervisor threatened to make her life more difficult unless she agreed to wear shorter skirts. The court decided that the employer was responsible for sexual harassment by its employees. The company was formally informed that they could defend themselves if they could satisfy the court that it had a well-publicized sexual harassment policy against such conduct. In conclusion, the employee failed to take advantage of the policy.

Case 2: June 1998—Faragher v. City of Boca Raton: A female lifeguard filed a charge stating that she had been harassed over several years with foul comments and offensive touching by other male lifeguards. Ms. Faragher was unaware of the complaint procedure to follow. The court determined that the City of Boca Raton was liable for the misconduct of its employees. The City failed to disseminate its policy against sexual harassment to beach employees.

The two cases decided by the Supreme Court are considered landmark decisions. The decisions of these two cases essentially had the Supreme Court re-writing the law referring to sexual harassment. The following was established in concern to an employer's responsibility:

1. Employers are responsible for harassment conduct by their managerial/supervisory employees.

2. When sexual harassment leads to an unfavorable employment action by the employer, for example, a demotion or a termination, the employer's liability is absolute.

3. When there has been no tangible action, the employers have the right to defend themselves only if they can prove that they have assumed reasonable care and taken reasonable steps to prevent and correct any sexual harassment. The employer must have a sexual harassment policy and complaint procedure.

4. If the employee unreasonably fails to take advantage of any preventive or corrective opportunities provided.

Sexual harassment charges can prove to be complicated. For more information about *sexual harassment* contact:

9to5, National Association of Working Women
614 Superior Avenue, NW
Cleveland, OH 44113
(800) 522-0925 (24-hour—7 day per week)

'9to5' is a national nonprofit organization. Its major tenants provide counseling, information, referrals for specific problems on the job that include pregnancy disability, family leave, termination, compensations, job discrimination, and sexual harassment. Free information is offered in both English and Spanish. The organization also offers a publication and newsletter.

14

UNPROFESSIONAL MANAGEMENT
"Jane's Story"

Interview: About a year ago, Jane was employed as the MainCoordinator at a prestigious women's club. To her, the job was easy and fun. Jane loved being around people, especially ones that enjoyed the amenities of a full programmed salon. Little did Jane know, she was in for the challenge of her life?

Each day Jane would report to work, only to find a member or members upset about something the director failed to do. It was like a merry-go-round, spinning faster and faster as each day came and went. What should have been a fun-filled job, turned into a ghastly experience.

The director called a meeting of middle management, which included the Aquatic Instructor, Beauty Salon Director, and the Main-Coordinator. It seems the word around the club was that the estaticians (Massage, Facial, Hair removal professionals) were stealing the club blind. The accounting department showed the director the financials from the last six months in which high numbers of members used the spas services, but with the books posting major losses.

This is where Jane reported the first major error. Instead of sitting at the meeting and allowing the director to talk, she interrupted by stating it was not the estatican's fault, but the club's management. Jane continued to say; the former main coordinator designed a sweet deal for these two employees. Then she laughed and added, and why not, one of the employees was his daughter. All the director had to do to rectify the situation, was restructure the contract.

To Jane, it seemed like a simple managerial task that the director should perform. According to Jane, the director did not agree it was his responsibility. He then quickly delegated the restructuring of the plan to the Main Coordinator, which of course, was Jane. She immediately could see where this was going, and jumped into the conversation by offering some advice. It seems the decision to cut an employee's pay should come directly from the top, and not middle management. Then she reminded the director, that her position was clearly classified, middle management.

The more advice Jane offered, the worst the situation became. Jane sighed and said, "Why did I open my mouth when I knew from past experience any advice offered would not be welcomed. But that's me, trying to do my job." She knew one of the employees in question had been there for a long time and was well liked by many of the members. It was obvious this employee would not be ecstatic when informed, her pay check would be considerably decreased, due to the fact, the club was not making money in the spa department. Jane knew a palace coupe was about to take place. She was also keen to the fact; she would probably end up taking the blame.

Jane sprung out of her chair and started pacing up and down the floor. She finally settled down and explained, "Sure shooting, the next week both of the employees were up in arms about their pay decreases." The two employees cornered the director as he was sneaking out the main clubhouse. They demanded to know the reason for their pay decreases. After he calmed them down, he casually informed them, "You see, Jane is in charge and you both need to talk with her. After hearing this, the two employees marched down to Jane's office. Jane said they both ranted and raved for an hour. It was very frustrating for she could not get in a word edge wise, and the two employees were not giving her a chance to explain. When they finally realized they were not getting anything accomplished by shouting at Jane, they marched back up to the director's office and demanded to be reinstated. Of course, the answer came back as a "No, I can't do that. You see Jane made the decision, and as the director, I have to back her one hundred percent."

Instead of the situation dying down liked the director had hoped, the two employees riled up the vocal contingency of members. The next thing Jane knew was ten of these members were storming her office screaming and accusing her of causing trouble for their friends. She said in exasperation, "I got to the point where I could not, or would not, take any more abusive treatment." These screaming meanies were not only rudely vulgar, but down right vicious.

Meanwhile back at the director's office, an emergency meeting was called. Top management (the director) decided to fire the two employees. Instead of arranging individual meetings face to face, the director called each one around eleven o'clock pm. He informed each one that there services would no longer be required at the club, and they need not report to work the next day, for they were officially fired. Obviously, this proved to be a poor managerial move, for one of the employees had dual responsibilities at the club. The young lady was contracted to teach several aerobic classes. In addition, the director did not inform Jane that he fired the two employees. This placed Jane in a difficult position. She did not find out until the next morning, she did not have an instructor to teach the most popular and best-attended aerobic class at the club.

Once again, the members became justifiably riled up, and stormed Jane's office. They accussed her of everything they could think of, and without mincing words. With the director's mishandling of the situation, he subtly allowed the members to vent their frustrations on Jane.

To my surprise as interviewer, Jane started laughing hysterically and described the whole situation as when the town's people carrying torches were storming Count Dracula's castle. I was amazed that Jane could sit during the interview, relate a serious story, only to find elements of humor.

Early the next day, one of the employees (former daughter of Jane's predecessor) arrived at the club to clean out her locker. As she was completing this task, one of the board of directors walked by and openly accussed her of stealing club property. The employee's friends gathered around once again, and were ready to lynch the outspoken board member.

Jane added, all this could have been avoided if the director had acted in a professional manner. First of all, you don't fire a long-time employee over the telephone and late at night. Secondly, the director should have arranged with the employee when she could return to the club. At that time, he would supervise the cleaning out of her locker. Since the director was clueless as how to act, WWIII broke out.

Action: Jane decided since this was an ongoing club occurrence, there obviously would not be any changes at any future date. The director was not going to change, and without his managerial support, she would be like Joan of Arc fighting for a cause, but then ending up being burned at the stake. Jane gave two weeks notice and moved on to another job.

Recourse: There is not a lot Jane could have done. The director did not break any laws being inept at his job. Although she should have seen clues during staff meetings as to the director's managerial skills. Warnings were clearly there, Jane unfortunately did not heed them

15

SCAPEGOAT
"Susan's Story"

Descriptive Analysis: The lack of strong support from top management is universally the number one barrier to quality and efficiency of staff. Most managers view the importance of an employee's commitment and hard work, but fail to acknowledge the importance of their own role.

There are indicators that will identify weak management. The problem is that most people accept the position, predicated on the information offered by management in the interviewing process. Until the individual actually becomes involved in the job, it is impossible to know what type of support will be offered from the top. By then it is too late, the individual has already made a commitment.

The manager/employee relationship problem is characterized by managers who blame and pass problems on to their employees. When facing dilemmas, these types of managers hide from the problem(s). Although upper management may feel the problems do not merit any status of importance. By isolating themselves from the employees, they slowly destroy morale and erode working relationships. This type of behavior by management transmits the message to employees; upper management is not going to support efforts when needed.

Interview: After twenty-five years of marriage, Susan never thought she would find herself alone. She knew they were drifting apart, but was shocked when Bill came home one day from the office only to announce, he wanted out of the marriage. Two months later, and a nasty court fight, Susan found herself sitting and wondering what she was going to do with the rest of her life. Her children were married with families of their own and would absolutely detest having grandma visiting daily. So instead of becoming a bothersome fifty year old, Susan decided to take an alternate action and register for classes at the nearby college.

Three years later, Susan finished her Masters degree and was hoping to land a teaching position at the college. The last three years had given her time to recoup emotionally from the divorce. Working on the degree gave her a purpose to get up in the morning and get through the day. Susan was also hoping to find someone special she could develop a relationship with at the university, but for some reason that never happened.

After completing the last requirement for the degree, Susan's first stop was the chairperson's office in the Department of Special Education. As she sat in the office waiting for Dr. Peterson to enter, she wondered if there were any possibilities of employment. Five minutes into the conversation with Dr. Peterson, she realized the writing on the wall. "You see Susan, it is quite unusual for the college to hire a recent graduate. I strongly recommended that if you want to pursue a teaching position that you apply at another institution."

Susan recalled that all she saw were Dr. Peterson's lips moving, she mentally shut him out. As he continued fabricating lame excuses for not hiring her, Susan could feel the red seep into her throat and up into her face. Interesting enough and very unlike Susan, she found herself standing up in the middle of Dr. Peterson's justification of why the college should not and could not hire her. Susan said she looked him straight in the eyes and firmly said: "If you can't hire me, then how did Jonathon (cohort-colleague, graduated with Susan) get his position?" Susan at that moment was hurt, angry and disappointed. She said I completely amazed myseld in what I said next; "Is it because Jonathon fits into your good ole boy system?" In a disgusting tone, she told Dr. Peterson, " You don't have to answer that, I already know you will concoct a few more feable excuses." Peterson appeared shocked and in a pleading tone begged Susan to sit back down. Obligingly she sat down to waited to hear what he had to say next. "Susan I hope this little conversation we are having is not going to cause problems. What I mean is it 's quite obvious that you are somewhat angry." Susan replied indignantly, "Why shouldn't I be, I worked hard for my degree and I feel I should be given a chance along with everyone else." Peterson pleadingly asked Susan to calm down. She knew at that momemt he was more concerned about his own well being. After clearing his throat Peterson lowered his voice and said, "You aren't going to take legal action are you?" On that note, Susan stood without responding and with a cold glare on her face, turned and left.

"Hm...legal action...tempting." With a glint in her eyes, she looked at me and admitted that the idea had crossed her mind. But to no avail for where she was in life, pursueing a legal rememdy to her was not worth the trouble. Although she admitted, "I think I made Peterson so nervous that he had to change his underwear. Now, that was worth the trouble."

On the way home she started wondering how smart it was to burn a bridge. Then flippantly decided, "Hey, there was no bridge of opportunity in the first place." Still, she felt disappointed in herself for the way she reacted. That evening having dinner with a friend, Susan related the conversation she had earlier with Dr. Peterson. Two glasses of wine later, she started laughed hysterically and admitted, "I truly enjoyed the response I gave the old boy, you should have seen the look on his face. It was absolutely priceless."

Six months elapsed and still no possibility of a job. One of her friends advised her to try a different field. "Why stay in Special Education where the pay is low and there are few opportunities? Listen since you are single why don't you consider moving north? It is common knowledge that educational opportunities are scarce here in the south." Susan thought to herself; that would be out of the question for her children and grandchildren lived here; she wasn't about to move thousand miles away.

The Sunday paper arrived and Susan found herself rummaging through the employment section. Right in front in big bold letters was a middle manager's position in a nearby country club. The responsibilities were to be in charge of three departments. The primary duties were to develop programs for adults and children. Right away, she thought this would be perfect, and telephoned the club to set-up an interview.

Two days later, she was sitting in the general manager's office. He seemed pleased she had an extensive educational background, but had reservations that he freely admitted. His major concern with Susan was that she may be too over qualified for the position, and he was rather dumbfounded as to why she was applying. Susan knew deep down she could not tell him, that after graduation it was impossible to find a job. What would he think? Contemplating a witty response, instead Susan calmly informed him, "This type of work is what I enjoy doing in life." The general manager appeared to accept the reason and continued to explain the required duties. He emphasized the importance of member relations, "Remember Susan, the club member must be highly respected and treated similar to demagogues. The key to operating a successful club that is owned by the members is to make them feel like royalty." Although he failed to tell Susan, taking member's abuse was part of the job.

The beginning date of employment was agreed upon, Susan arrived promptly at nine a.m. only to find that the general manager was off on vacation. The initial agreement was to meet the general manager the first day of work, where he would orientate Susan with all departments and areas. Oh well she thought, I am a professional and should be able to conduct myself accordingly. Susan walked from department to department introducing herself as the new program coordinator. Everyone seemed receptive and gracious.

The next step was off to her office where she received another unexpected surprise. The original office set-up was changed, now she would be sharing an office with one other person. Susan also was not informed; her office would be open to the rest of the staff. This constituted around twenty arriving and departing part-time employees, all using her office. It appeared to be grand central station; privacy was out of the question.

In the middle of my next question, Susan raised her hand in a time-out signal, motioning that she had one other comment to share. "Remember, the office the general manager promised with the nice bay window, well it turned out to be a cement, jammed pack broom closet." OK, she thought to herself, I can handle this, but it is starting to bother me that everything promised in the original meeting is changing drastically. It felt like the old bait and switch routine. But the wrose was soon to come and that was with the arrival of Jimmy-John. A shrt,squatty bodied man came barging into Susan's office announcing his name and informing Susan right up front that he was a good friend with the general manager. "You see little lady, I am real good friends with the general manager. I just want you to know that how things were run in the past would continue the same in the future. Susan unable to withhold her merriement as to the scene in front of her replied: "I really don't know the history of events that happened in the past, but would be grateful to be informed as to any set-in stone procedures that need to be followed. Jimmy-Johns then turned proudly toward her and said in his redneck accent, "Remember, I am the general manager's number one guy. That's how it always been and how it's going to continue." Well thought Susan, as least I am learning the hierarchical pecking order early in the game.

The first day seemed uneventful except for the fitness director's declaration that he was the top man on the totem pole. The only thing he did not ask me to do was to refer to him as "your highness." Susan using her dry humor put her hand up in the air and said, "Stop don't order yet, for this story gets better by the day.

Susan was sitting in her office when she received a telephone call from the general manager. He apologized profusely stating that he had forgotten about his vacation, but assumed that Jimmy-John helped acclimate her to her surroundings. Susan replied Jimmy John was more than helpful and even though it was only the second day, she felt quite comfortable.

The general manager continued to say, the second reason he was calling was that he forgot to tell Susan about a situation that needed her immediate attention. Eager to please, Susan said whatever needs to be done she would be more than happy to do. He continued on saying, "There is a problem at the club, you see only club members are allowed on the property, you know because of insurance and all." Susan agreed. The general manager then explained the public and private schools were dropping off their students in the parking lot by the front gate. Then he added indignantly, and on club property. The General Manager requested Susan to figure out how to disband the dropping off of the students at the club. It would entail her finding a new drop-off place down the street. Remember Susan, the General Manager continued, "Some of the member's children are dropped off at the club. They probably will not be happy their children will no longer be allowed to disembark the school bus on our property. A good alternative would be; If they are dropped off down the street, the member's children can walk back to use the club." Susan then politely interrupted and said that in reviewing the club's by-laws, paragraph five on page ten, "Members' children under the age of sixteen are not allowed to be at the club unattended. After Susan finished there was a long pause on the other end, finally the General Manager replied, "Well yes Susan, but that is something you will have to figure out and deal with."

The next two days Susan worked around the clock trying to come up with a solution, no matter which way she turned, nothing seemed right. She decided to telephone a friend about her dilemma and bounce off a few ideas. Susan's friend stopped her in the middle of the conversation and asked, "Why are you in charge of this situation, and why wasn't the General Manager handling it? This thought had occurred to Susan, but being brand new, she wanted to prove wanted to prove her professionalism at being able to handle any situation. Her friend agreed, the first step Susan needed to take was to contact the superintendent and head masters of the schools. She needed to explain the insurance liability the club was undertaking by allowing member and non-member students to be dropped off on the club's property. The friend then added, "Susan you will have to put up with disgruntled members, remember how convenient it was for them to have the school bus drop off their kid(s) and let the employees at the club act as babysitters, until they decided to pick them up. What her friend meant was that these members were used to the convenience of not having to pick-up their children and cart them to the club for after-school activities.

It was well known by long standing employees; as to the damage, these kids would do to the club's property. Several of the kids planted sharp objects in the flowerbeds, broke the mirrors in the aerobics room, defaced the walls in the bathrooms, etc.

After Susan contacted the schools, she was pleasantly pleased the schools agreed with her. Most of the school contacts she spoke with could never understand why the club allowed their property to be a drop-off and pick-up destination. Susan thought everything was going along smoothly, and then the telephone calls started.

Members started calling and blaming Susan for changing the rules. They even went as far as threatening to get her fired. In her charming southern way, Susan explained the liability the club would incur if an accident happened. Standing out in the parking lot one afternoon, she saw four near misses of children being hit by automobiles. Susan looked at me and in a southern business like tone said, "It was an accident waiting to happen."

One week passed with the general manager returning from his vacation. The first thing he did was to request Susan to meet him in his office. As she sat in his office she wondered why the urgency, but then realized he was upset with members calling and complaining about the bus situation.

Susan looked him straight in the eyes and reminded him that he ordered her to take care of the situation. She felt the majority of members understood and were abiding accordingly, it was unfortunate a few were upset, but that was to be expected. The General Manager in a sarcastic tone said, "yea, I know only too well, because three members already called and complained as to how you are taking care of the situation." Shock set-in and Susan started defending herself, but abruptly stopped. She realized by the look on the General Managers' face, nothing said would change his opinion.

Next, the telephone rang, Susan thought this would be a reprieve, but then realized it was one of the three disgruntled members. The General Manager bent over backwards apologizing for the past two days school bus fiasco. At times, he seemed strong, but then just when she was starting to get confidence in him, he would back down and redirect the blame to Susan.

The next two weeks, neither Susan nor any other employee at the club saw the manager. He would arrive at the club early in the morning, close his door, and leave late at night. He even went so far as to have his meals delivered by his personal secretary.

This was the beginning of what Susan knew was going to be a hard road to travel. For she knew after the first week's events, her position as program developer was really a cover-up. It was merely a scapegoat position, intended to cover the weak General Manager's inability to perform his job.

Action: There was very little what Susan could do in this situation. The only option was to resign and move on to another job. She could request an exit interview where she would have a format to express her feelings. All this may result in is a catharsis (way to relieve frustration by talking about the causes of the problems) for Susan.

Susan did request an exit interview. After the interview, she never heard from anyone from the company again. Although six months later she heard through a friend, the General Manager was replaced.

Recourse: How to evaluate top management:

1. Listen to how the manager reacts to questions

2.   Observe how the manager reacts in board meetings

Without a communication system within an organization, the infra-structure will appear and be disjointed. If the manager hides in his/her office, and there is no dialogue, employees will get the message that their input is not important. This will lessen the levels of efficiency. In addition, if there is no communication from the top, there is usually a lack of dialogue between departments.

16

OVERQUALIFIED
"Laura's Story"

Descriptive Analysis: There are misconceptions concerning individuals that earn advanced college degrees. Many people feel in order to earn a Ph.D.; you have to be a genius. Please note, the information offered in this interview is also useful for Master of Arts (MA) and Master of Science (MS) graduates. Due to this attitude, prospective employers treat these individuals differently. They are under the assumptions, this type of person is going to demand more money, or more benefits, and insist on a higher status level/title.

There is a stigma Ph.D.'s are cursed with, employer's view them as individuals, who have spent three to four years in academia, and now are unable to adjust to the demands of a commercial environment. Therefore, these same employers are readily seen hiring inexperienced-fledglings, fresh out of college.

It is a subtle warning when in an interview; the employer states, he or she feels you are overqualified for the job. Many times employers are apprehensive and are leery due to the individual's highly attained educational level. The employer's feeling is that the degreed individual may not be challenged to the fullest and experience boredom in the job. This may result in a high turn over, low level of productivity, or both.

Interview: Laura is around fifty-one years old, but no one would ever know it by looking at her. In walked Laura sporting a super short hair-do, running shorts, t-shirt, and Nike's. The only time one could estimate her true age was when she laughed, and then little creases around her eyes folded neatly in. Otherwise, one would think, they were looking at a thirty-something year old.

Here is Laura's story. Two months into the job as executive director for an exclusive health spa, Laura was scheduled to attend the national convention in Chicago. On the last night of the convention, Laura sat next to the director of operations from the same spa where she was employed. About half way through the dinner and totally out of the blue, the operations director looked at Laura and informed her that he was going to do her a favor and let her know why she was a failure. He continued to say: "I have been meaning to tell you Laura form the first day you arrived that your precious, hotty-totty Ph.D. means nothing around here. All it signals is that you are too intelligent for this job, which according to you gives you a license to run your mouth and be outspoken at the wrong time. And that simply sums it up as to why many of the spa guests honestly do not like you." Very little catches Laura off-guard, but this one was close. She took a long deep breath, sat back and crossed her arms in readiness for battle. Laura was in no mood to tolerate such trivial dribble and especially from someone she totally disrespected. Instead of dismissing his comment, she turned directly to confront him by replying, "Having a usable brain is an asset and not a people relation deterrent, but he wouldn't know." Yes, it was true, Laura had earned her doctorate three years previous, but anyone that knew her would verify that she never used the degree as a crutch or a weapon to be thrown in someone's face. In other words she was not the type of person to wear her degree on her sleeve.

An uneasy quiet settled over the table. You could see some of the people start to squirm nervously in their chairs. Then the ops-director came back for round two. He strongly suggested that Laura should change her ways and join a fundamentalist organization in which he belonged. Not believing her ears, she firmly warned him to back off, and leave her alone. Instead of taking her advice he started pontificating as to the virtues she could expound from this wonderful organization. Reaching the height of frustration and realizing he would not back off and leave her alone, she rose to her feet, excused herself from the table and returned to her hotel room. Immediately shs found herself phoning her husband Bill and in sort of a semi-shock trance explained what had occurred. "Listen Laura you have known for a long time what a jerk that guy can be...why are you so surprised now? Ok, try to calm down, order a nice dinner through room service, take a nice bath, and go to bed. After twenty-five years of marriage, Bill still knew what to do and what to say. "Holy heavens…I love that man" Laura churned in."

Returning to the spa, the incident was still upsetting Laura. One of her strong holds was her ability to deal with people, and she knew that. Her husband used to joke with her, "Laura; your true calling is running for political office. You could convince Eskimos to buy snow from you… everyone would vote for you and not even know why…."

After wrestling with the incident for about a week, she arranged a meeting with the supervisor of the spa. The strangest thing happened whenever she met with this man, "you see" Laura said almost cautiously, "he would sit in this big leather chair staring out the window and hardly ever look at me or make eye contact." So there she was, pouring out her story in hopes the general manager could make a suggestion as what to do, since she had to share an office with this operations director. Especially now that she intensely despised him; made every day life even more intolerable.

This was as much as she could swallow, according to Laura and in her own words this limp, little jerk of a supervisor that used her in the past as a scapegoat due to his inability to perform his job, was sitting there accusing her of not having people skills. "Who in the world does he think he is…Mr Personality! " No way was Laura going to sit and take that idiotic abuse. To make matters even worse the general manager then said, "I would like to set you straight about the operation director's fundamentalist program. I know you think it is a cult an I personally resent the inference. Kicking herself in the foot, Laura said I should not have told the general manager that I researched the organization on the Internet. I found a report that even the US government classifies it as a cult with a warning for people to be careful.

Laura realized what was going on for she was amazed the supervisor used the same verbage as the operations director used in Chicago, just one week before. It sounded like a tape recording being played back.

However, it was not difficult in putting two and two together, realizing the supervisor was being manipulated by the operations director through this fundamentalist movement. She recalled some of the employees talking about how the supervisor and the operations director attended meetings off spa property. This was not one meeting but four to five each week.

Laura looked at the supevisorand broke out into a state of uncontrollable laughter. Trying to regain her composure, she literally jumped to her feet, and quickly exited the room.

Bill, being involved in the corporate world for more than two decades would not allow Laura to merely walk away. He insisted that she arrange an exit interview with the regional manager. Laura confided that she did this merely to placate Bill, for she knew the regional manager andThow he worked. Laura stated that it was a total waste of time for this guy was the quintessential paradigm of the good ole boy. She said I could predict what would happen in the interview. The regional manager would pretend to be interested and promise to take action to rectify the situation. What is the saying: the checkis in ithe mail…interesting enough, a lie that my grandfather used in his day is still being used today.

Action: Laura elected to go through an exit interview. After the interview, there was no further communication with anyone from the company.

Recourse: If the individual is viewed by the prospective employer as:

- Overly Academic

- Too Intelligent

- Too Expensive

- Too Over qualified

Then it may best for the individual to heed these possible problematic signs and seek employment elsewhere.

If a person decides to pursue the position, then it is best to remember that the employer may not view the advanced degrees with the same importance as the individual. It is critical to emphasize skills rather than specific knowledge during the initial interview. The task to be accomplished is to convince the employer, the individual will be an asset to the company.

17

SET TO FAIL
"Kate's Story"

Descriptive Analysis: It is important for an individual to carefully document 'all' work related circumstances. The individual should retain one copy, where another copy should be placed in the company's personnel file. This action is to protect the individual in the event a future employer asks for a reason or reasons an individual left the previous place of employment. If the former employer tries to demean the individual by falsifying the reasons for termination or dismissal, the individual has a documented recourse of action.

Interview: Kate decided that after her son entered elementary school, the timing would be perfect for her to return to work. Before marrying Jack, she was the head assistant for the mayor of the city of Longwood, Illinois. Simply stated, Kate was the mayor's right arm. He literally did not make a move without her being involved. The pace was hectic with sixteen-hour days, but she admitted…she loved every minute of it.

Jack and Kate did not marry until late in life, and when Jason arrived, Kate was already in her forties. Waiting until her son was comfortable in school was difficult for Kate, but something she and Jack agreed upon before marriage.

Now was the time for her to start looking for a way to get back into the main stream of things, and once again become involved in her career. Unfortunately, they no longer resided in the same city where Kate was once employed which left very little networking opportunities. Jack had received a company promotion along with a relocation packet. Kate knew starting over in a brand new city was going to be a challenge, but she had no choice.

The planned community where they relocated had a country club. This club was primarily golf, but did have a small fitness center. In Longwood, Kate had previously taught a variety of exercise classes and was involved in planning club activities.

News spreads quickly in a small community. The country club's athletic director was fired. The reasons were never openly discussed, but rumors had it that there were some unsavory business transactions occuring. Even though the job was vacant for only a day, it was already being advertised in the local newspaper. The ad read as follows: Immediate opening for a qualified professional with expertise in the fitness field. The position requires strong organizational skills, and a creative ability. Kate felt and knew she was a perfect fit for the job, and called for an interview.

One week later the club's general manager called to arrange an interview time. Kate arrived at the interview fifteen minutes before the scheduled time. After checking in with the receptionist, she quietly sat down and thumbed through a magazine. The interview was scheduled for ten o'clock. Ten o'clock arrived, ten-fifteen, and by ten-twenty, Kate politely asked the receptionist if there was something wrong and wondered if the general manager was unable to keep the appointment. The receptionist in between smacking her gum coyly replied, "He would be here shortly." She also added in a whiney voice that this was typical for him when he had interviews scheduled. Around quarter to eleven, a heavyset man around the age of thirty-five entered the foyer. Kate realized immediately, this was the general manager.

She immediately stood-up and walked over and introduced herself. He responded pleasantly and asked her to come with him into his office. To her amazement, as soon as they entered the office he picked up the telephone and placed a call. Kate admitted that sitting in his office while he talked on the phone, made her quite uncomfortable. She wondered how long this conversation, which seemed to be more personal than business, was going to continue. After what seemed like an hour, the general manager finally hung up the phone, and without even looking at her started the interview.

That night while lying in bed with Jack, Kate related how the interview went. Jack thought it was strange for Kate to comment three times, that it seemed strange, the general manager during the interview sat staring out the window. "He hardly ever looked at me", Kate said in exasperation. "Once in awhile, he would glance at me but then redirect his gaze." All Kate saw of this man was his profile. Jack asked her how that made her feel, and she quickly responded by saying, "it was nerve-wracking and made me start to perspire profusely." Thinking this was just his style; Kate dismissed the physical aspects of the interview, and went on to explain the responsibilities of the position.

Kate apprehensively admitted that what the general manager offered seemed rather unusual. The offer consisted of a substantially low-based salary, along with possibilities of earning high commissions. In other words, if she produced revenue-generating programs, the financial benefits would offset the low based salary.

Knowing the numerous opportunities at the club, Kate felt all that was needed was someone like her to develop programs. Understanding the club as well as she did, Kate knew there was a lot of work that had to be done before the revenue-generating programs would give her a substantial paycheck to take home. Unfortunately she was not initially told in the interview, her programs would not be given approval for implementation. She was being set-up to do the work at dirt pay, with false promises of a golden carrot dangling at the end of the line.

Being in the position for three months, Kate had the fitness area moving in the right direction. This was a major undertaking while at the same time keeping the members contented. The hours were long and tedious, but Kate kept thinking about the financial rewards she would reap from developing and implementing the programs. At the end of each day, Kate would take the last half hour and record the day's events. This task was not only to create a paper trail but gave her a sense of accomplishment. It was analogous to someone patting her on the back and telling her of the fine job she is doing.

Working for the mayor in Longwood helped Kate develop strong survival skills. She knew the utmost importance of keeping well-organized files. Her first self-directed assignment was to set-up a filing system that could easily be managed. Each file would have a comprehensive written report as to each project developed. Memos, letters, minutes of meetings, any type of communication would be recorded

In her previous job, she witnessed a few of her co-workers unable to get out of trouble due to the lack of backup documentation. One woman in particular that Kate recalled was accused of non-performance of assigned duties. Since she did not keep a log or a diary of her efforts, she was unable to present a case. Kate added; it was unfortunate, for I know for a fact this woman worked to full capacity. In some cases, she actually put in a 150% effort, compared to some of her slacker co-workers. "I was the only one that came forth and defended her. But without written documentation, it was hard to prove her innocence." Kate said she felt real bad when the woman was forced to resign, but there was nothing more she could do to help. According to Kate it was a valuable lesson learned. No matter how comfortable a person may be in a job; it is always smart to be prepared just in case things go wrong. Maintaining adequate backup documentation may seem time consuming; but it is well worth the effort. "I have to admit, by forcing myself to write everything down in print, keeps me organized. I also found myself thinking through projects with a newfound intensity and a keener eye to detail."

The fourth month at the job was just beginning, and Kate was starting to get a little excited now that the rudimentary work was completed. She would now have time to develop the programs that she felt would be positive for the club.

Late one afternoon as she was sitting in her office, the tennis pro walked in. The conversation in the beginning was filled with casual generalities and then finally got around to the specifics. Evidently he was uncomfortable with the changes Kate was instigating at the club. He coyly admitted in his own way the changes were necessary but wanted Kate to know the members were not happy. Kate calmly replied, "it is impossible to please all the people all the time, and that it seemed the majority were accepting the changes for they could see the accompanying benefits." The tennis pro announced in a pompous manner that the fitness center was not supposed to be a revenue-generating center. That it was originally planned in its inception to lose money. Kate realized that it was not the members that were dis-satisfied, but this middle-aged, underpaid tennis pro who was happy with the status quo. He was contented planning his own day, which usually consisted of three to four actual hours. Kate was perceptive enough to realize this man was giving her a subtle warning. He was telling her under no uncertain terms that she was causing problems for the other employees. All the changes made their jobsto appear less than adequate. Kate thought at the time, this disgruntled tennis pro would more than likey work behind the lines in an attempt to demean her work.

One thing was evident; Kate knew she had to be careful playing company politics. It was general knowledge, the tennis pro was embedded deeply into the clubs 'good ole boys system. It was common knowledge that he went out several times during the week and drank beer with the general manager. So in essence, the general manager and the tennis pro were 'buddies.'

One night Kate was explaining to Jack, "If I don't make the changes, I will not be able to develop the programs I was originally hired to do." Jack commented, " I don't like the relationship between the general manager and the tennis pro." He continued to say, "He thought she may be caught in a catch twenty-two. No matter what programs you develop Kate; there will always be a certain degree of change when implemented.

"The difficulty you are going to run into is that every time you attempt to introduce a new program, theis tennis pro will make it a point to stand in your way. If you complain to the General Manager about his favorite drinking buddy, you and I both know, it will not be well received." Kate sighed and asked Jack, "What am I going to do?" I need those new programs in order to generate revenues. If not, there will not be paycheck and this job will become a total farce. "I don't know, It is just too difficult to work as hard as I have been, especially without a monetary reward to show for it."

Kate remained in the position for three more months, receiving a paycheck of little more than minimum pay. One day after a member stormed out of her office screaming at her for something she was not responsible for, and then realizing that the tennis pro was behind the incident, she knew it was time to resign.

That night Jack paced up an down the floor while listening to Kate explain how she felt. "Yes, she was angry, and felt she had a right to be." Jack knew she needed to vent in order to flush the anger out of her system. After she finally collapsed backward onto the couch in mere exhaustion, Jack started to explain that it was not her fault. He knew the professional job she had been doing, and the reason she stayed as long as she did. Nevertheless, the cards were stacked against her, and the smartest move she could make at this point, was to leave. "Go on to bigger and better things Kate. You have all the ability in the world; don't let a petty, aging tennis pro get the best of you. Pass him by."

Kate explained to Jack that the six months of hard work she had put in at the club, resulted in a total waste of time. How was she going to explain to her next employer that she was set-up and used. She would only come across as a disgruntled female, one that did not get her way in her previous job. The question Kate said she was struggling with was; should she put this experience on her resume', or just forget it never happened.

Action: Even with Kate's extensive paper trail, she did not have any type of legal action to pursue. She had to accept that she was a victim of circumstances, things that sometimes happen to individuals in business. Before completely accepting the premise that fate had thrown her a bad curve, Kate needed closure. In order for her to mentally deal with the situation, she made a copy of her paper documentation along with a copy of her personnel file (one of her secretarial friends secretly transported out of the office). She desperately wanted to end the whole experience. Without telling Jack, she sent all her documentation to the corporate office. That was the end for Kate. Although six months later, a friend phoned with a message that the General Manager and tennis pro were both fired. After the call, Kate shared a thought with Jack that it was a down right shame for true professionals to be run off and then when corporate finally takes action, it's too late.

Jack encouraged Kate to put the work related experience on her resume'. "Use it as a stepping-stone, a way for you to land a job working with real professionals. Do not let time go unaccounted, but use every moment wisely. Think about it as making a silk purse out of a pig's ear. If you put in the valuable time, then take credit for it. Kate had to laugh for Jack sometimes had a real way of expressing himself.

Three weeks after Kate resigned from the club, she interviewed for a similar position she previously had when they lived in Illinois. Some stories do have happy endings for Kate is now the senior administrative coordinator for Senator Ted. L. Burns.

Recourse: Maintaining a paper trail is an absolute must for survival in any workplace. The following should be included in this (diary) type documentation: Note: include date on each entry

1. Performance reviews

2. Commendations or Reprimands

3. Salary increases or decreases

4. Informal comments made by your employer in reference to your work

Record:

     1. Date

     2. Time

3. Location of event(s)

4. Which members of management were involved/present

5. Any witnesses present (names)

6. Written information given by the employer as to changes in the workplace

Unfair Disciplinary Notice: If by chance the individual receives an unfair disciplinary notice, there are specific steps that may be taken:

1. Understand the reason for the notice of behavior

2. Review the company's handbook as to policy clarification in reference to such behavior

3. If the individual is confused as to the company's policy, a meeting with the supervisor or human resource representative may be requested as for clarification

4. Organize memos, brochures, written evaluations, or employee orientation videos that illustrate any commendations or criticisms of the individual's work.

5. Preview the personnel file and make copies of all reviews and reports

18

SURVIVING IN THE WORKPLACE WITH EEOC CHARGES
"Ellen's Story"

Descriptive Analysis: In 1996, a large fortune 500 company (which will not be named) became involved in extensive legal problems. Twenty-nine female employees filed sexual harassment charges with the EEOC against the company. It was since reported, more than half of the twenty-nine women who filed the *harassment charges* against the company have been fired or have had to leave due to *harassment*. These women not only lost decent paying jobs, but also health insurance and pension benefits.

The story does not end there, unfortunately these women are being retaliated against in finding new employment opportunities simply because they wanted their former employer to stop breaking the law.

The majority of the managerial staff was well aware of the *sexual harassment* going on at the company. The women involved in filing the *charge,* face continual harassment and financial ruin. Certain employees that filed private lawsuits have also reported incidences of hostile acts and death threats.

The filing of sexual harassment charges was not a difficult decision for these women to make, for the blatant sexual harassment that occurred everyday reached a point of intoleration. Unfortunately, these women were not ready for the actions the company took in *retaliation*. Here are some of the actions that transpired:

- The *hostile work place* caused several women to become physically ill due to the stress and the physical abuse.

- Stressful financial circumstances arose due the company withholding disability benefits

- A few of the unemployment *claims* challenged by female employees who previously had no problems locating jobs, now were suddenly unable to find decent work.

- Many of the women had to accept jobs far below their training and education levels.

- Several of the female employees are reported to be in serious financial trouble and face bankruptcy.

The message is clear from the above information; even though you may have a strong case, be ready for unfair play. Most companies will not accept sexual *harassment charges* or any other kind of charges brought against them. In other words, be ready for a fight, for most companies will not lie down and concede their guilt. Even though it may seem like an open and closed case, the accused most likely will put up some sort of defense.

Interview: Knowing she had been treated unfairly at work, Ellen was at a total loss as to her legal rights and recourse. She shared that it was difficult enough trying to conjure up enough energy in the morning so she could arrive at work with a positive attitude. She felt hurt, but at the same time was afraid to say anything for fear of losing her job. Ellen shared, "I don't know if I can land another good paying job. Even though she did not look fifty-nine years old, she knew a future employer would be able to figure out her age from her resume'.

"Ok, let's start at the beginning. "You see", Ellen said, the rest of the staff knew I had requested a promotion, and why not, I had been with the company for five years and during that time received excellent reviews

News travels quickly around a office. It was almost as though the walls had ears. What struck Ellen as being unusual was that some of her co-workers whom she had lunch with on a regular basis and shared some fun times discussing family and kids, started to treat her differently. It was almost as though she had concocted a rare disease. She started to laugh and then added, "I now know how people with leoparcy felt."

Ellen sat for a moment in silence, shaking her head, appearing to rationalize what had happened. "What was wrong with trying to get ahead in life? Earning more income would really help at home, and many of co-workers knew that." Ellen continued to say that nothing had changed since she submitted her request to be interviewed for the higher position. She did not feel she changed in anyway, shape, or form. Now being black balled from a part of the group was disheartening.

Two months passed without a scheduled time for an interview. Finally, the day came when the manager requested her presence in his office. Feeling a surge of excitement, Ellen quickly dropped what she was doing and scurried up the stairs to his office. As soon as she entered the office, she could feel that the news was not going to be good, for the manager merely glanced in her direction when she walked in.

The first thing out of the manager's mouth was, "I don't feel you are qualified for the promotion.and even if you were it would not be good for the morale of the company." Ellen felt a surge of disappointment and sat speechless, for how long she had no idea. The manager finally responded by saying the position would be bettered suited for one of the younger male employees. Corporate for sometime has been preparing some of these young men for down the road managerial positions. "You see Ellen," the manager said in a demeaning tone, "The Company needs new, young blood to carry on. And some of the older personnel have to understand; that is life." Ellen's mind was racing, as soon as she collected her thoughts she looked the manager straight in the eyes and reminded him, "I don't need the intensive training the younger guys need, for I already am well versed in the product and have extensive experience in its marketing.

It was like talking to a wall, even though she knew she was the best qualified for the position. The manager would not hear of it, so therefore the promotion was completely out of the picture. Ellen silently stood up and left his office. Tears started to well up in her eyes and she knew without looking that the group of young managers were all watching. As she walked down the stairs to her office, she could feel all eyes upon her. At one point Ellen turned and saw three of the young guys talking and laughing. As soon as they saw her gaze, they turned abruptly away.

Not surprising, the next week the promotion went to a young guy, with no experience except for a six month stint in sales. Ellen lowered her head and in a quiet tone commented that she turned into the laughing stock of the company. The attitude of some of her co-workers was disheartening, "Who does she think she is trying for a position like that." As the days turned into weeks; things became worse and to the point where Ellen did not want to go to work.

Sitting quietly, Ellen turned her heat and looked out the window. She then calmly turned back towards me and said, "The reason I am sharing this experience with you is that the hurt turned into anger, and I know that if I don't do something about it, the anger will eventually affect my health."

According to Ellen, this anger stimulated her into telephoning a lawyer an inquiring as to what recourse, if any did she have? Attorney Charles Douglas was highly recommended and a partner with a reputable firm, one that was well known to be fair with their clients. The first thing Ellen said after she explained the situation, "How much, and what will the fee be?" Ellen knew most people (including herself) were afraid to talk to an attorney, even when they know they need one. The fear is real in that they may not be able to afford the legal fee.

In Ellen's case, her fears were dissuaded when she heard the attorney's response. Charles explained he would take a small percentage of the settlement, and if for some reason, they did not win; there would not be a bill. He continued to say, "I only take cases that I am sure there will be a positive judgment."

Charles suggested that Ellen organize all her memos and then plan an hour meeting with him in the law office. He was pleased when Ellen told him that she had kept a well organized and succinct paper trail of all incidents that occurred in the office, of course, with things that directly affected her. Charles then said that if the case makes it to a jury trial the paper trail will be a heaven sent.

Ellen started organizing the memos as soon as she hung up the telephone. A feeling of relief came over her when she realized how easy it was to accomplish this task. Thanks to Ellen's propensity to keep everything in order, each memo sent had the date clearly marked in the upper right hand corner. All she had to do was to arrange the memos in order according to the dates. After completing the project, she sat down and started reading through the paper trail that had accumulated over the past two years. Thinking back to the telephone conversation with Charles Douglas, she distinctly recalled the importance he placed on the memos and felt assured that the written documentation would well meet his standards.

The meeting with Charles was scheduled for Friday at noon. The first thing Ellen thought when she walked into the firm's lobby was "Oh my goodness, marble floors, marble desks, gold door knobs…help this smells expensive. Taking a deep breath, she walked over an introduced herself to the receptionist. As Ellen sat down, she kept repeating over and over again, remember if your case wins, the fee is automatically subtracted from the settlement. In addition, if you lose, there is no bill.

A short man, slightly balding and with a bit of a gut walked confidently into the reception area. Ellen knew immediately that was Charles Douglas. After saying something to the receptionist, he glanced over in Ellen's direction. With a big smile on his face, Charles walked over and held out his hand. Ellen felt a feeling of comfort spread over her body. Charles escorted her to the main conference room where they sat for the next hour discussing the merits of the case.

Everything seemed to run quite smoothly until Charles suggested that Ellen return to work. It was important she stay in her position while the EEOC claims were being filed. "Oh no, I can't Ellen said in a high pitched manner. " I just can't continue going back into that office and being constantly humiliated." Charles said he understood and knew it would not be easy, but it was important for the case. The reason for returning to work is that the case would appear stronger, especially if the manager forced Ellen into resigning.

Charles warned Ellen, "If you think things were bad at work before you filed the charges, be ready for worse things to happen. "But don't worry" Charles stated: "You have the law on your side." Management will appear to be walking on eggshells around you. Moreover, if management tries anything out of the ordinary, call my office immediately. My assistant Martha always knows where I am and how to get a hold of me. In other words Ellen, hang in there as long as you can.

Walking out of Charles's office, Ellen felt confident that she made the right choice. Instead of pushing the buttom for the elevator, she went directly to the ladies room. Pleased that no one was there using the facility, she looked directly into the mirror and said to outloud: "you did the right thing, for if management can do it to you, they will do it to anyone. Stand up and fight for your rights...you won't regret it."

The next week charges were filed. Ellen knew exactly when management was notified for the manager sequestered himself in his office for the entire day. He most likely was on the telephone with corporate counsel trying to figure out what to do in this situation. Being new to management, Ellen thought to herself that he never had to deal with such a situation, and probably was clueless as what steps needed to be taken. Tuesday morning when Ellen walked into her office, the phone rang with the secretary requesting her immediate presence in the manager's office. When she walked in, the manager was positioned behind his desk with the comptroller standing behind him. The manager glared at Ellen with great disdain and silently gestured for her to be seated. As soon as Ellen sat down, the manager pushed a stack of legal documents in her direction and demanded her to sign them. In an admonishing tone, he told her she had to choice but to cooperate. Ellen remembered what Charles had said, "don't sign anything." Charles also told her that she did not have to put up with such abusive treatment and did not have to engage in a discourse with these people. To management's surprise, Ellen reached in her pocket and pulled out her mobile phone and quickly dialed Charles's number. Martha answered the telephone and informed Ellen that Charles was not in his office. Ellen then proceeded to explain that she was enlisted to report to the manager's office where the comptroller and the manager were attempting to coerce her into signing documents. Martha told Ellen, "do not sign anything, for I will get in touch with Charles immediately. Keep your mobile phone on, Charles will be calling you in a few minutes. " Ellen stood up and politely excused herself from the manager's office.

Martha quickly added, "keep your mobile phone on..." Five minutes later the phone rang with Charles on the line congratulating her for being strong and doing the right thing. Remember, the longer you hang in there the stronger the case will be.

The next week did not bring any surprises; Ellen seemed mentally prepared for any thing out of the ordinary that management could contrive. When the work schedule came out, she wound up with a double shift resulting in a fourteen-hour day. Her workload also increased with subtle demands on deadlines.

Ellen freely admitted, one of the most difficult things to do was not having the freedom to share with anyone what was happening. At times, she wanted to scream, but would stop, take a deep breath and remind herself that this nightmare would soon be over. No matter the outcome, she was going to quit the job, but this time not without a fight. In order to keep her sanity, she would constantly remind herself as how management mistreated her.

There were times when Ellen said she was ready to jump out a window. What she really wanted was to desperately talk with someone about what was happening. The only person she thought she could turn to that would understand what she was going through was surprisingly, her ex-husband.

Jonah and Ellen had divorced three years ago after thirty years of marriage, five kids, and three dogs. It was not a bad marriage; probably the best way to describe the relationship was; there wasn't one. Jonah did his own thing while Ellen in turn did hers. When he was not working, he was off with the boys on a fishing or hunting trip. Ellen admitted that in desperation she found other interests in which she became deeply involved.

The divorce was amicable as is their friendship now. Therefore, Jonah was the obvious one to call. Up until now, he had no idea what was happening. With his slow, deliberte, laid-back Texas drawl, Jonah answered the phone on the second ring. Without exchanging a common greeting. Ellen blurted out, "Jonah I need help, I need to talk to you." Without any hesitation, Jonah replied: "no problem…when and where?" Ellen thought it would be a good idea if they could meet after work at her apartment. The last thing she wanted was for someone to over hear their conversation.

Jonah arrived exactly at six o'clock wearing his ten-gallon hat and genuine leather cowboy boots. Even though she had not seen him in about a year, the only difference was a little more gray in his beard. He still had that glint in his blue eyes when he smiled and for a brief moment wondered why they divorced. However, she hastily dismissed the thought.

As soon as Jonah sat down, Ellen thrust a beer into his hand. Jonah replied: "just like old times, get me drunk and then take advantage of me." They both laughed. "No, I need your expert advice and don't want any craziness." Ellen started from the beginning explaining what events led up to the present. Jonah sat patiently listening to every word, not commenting, but merely nodding his head from time to time.

After she finished, Ellen broke down and starting sobbing. Instead of Jonah sitting passively, he stood up, came over to her, and gave her a long enduring hug. "don't worry," he said, "you have every right in the world to proceed with this. You were passed over for a position you were clearly qualified for by a younger- inexperienced guy. Then to pour salt on the wound, the manager told you that you're too old for the job. If that is not enough grounds to sue, I don't know what is. I want you to contact an attorney as soon as possible. I have this gut feeling that you are going to win." Looking like the cat that swallowed the canary, Jonah turned and smiling proudly announced: "I have to tell you, I am proud of you girl...I always knew you had it in you. If there is anything I can do to help, just ask."

Ellen feeling a sense of relief, smiled and thanked him. "Jonah, you don't know how much you have helped just by listening to me." Thinking back, Ellen thought if there could have been more times shared like this, maybe we would still be together. But no, first things first, concentrate on the present.

The weekend produced a much-needed escape from the turmoil and tension of the previous week. The staff meeting on Friday seemed filled with a strange air of tension. Maybe knowing what the situation was made Ellen a little more paranoid. Every time the manager made a comment, she felt it was directed at her. Thinking back over the events of the past week, Ellen wondered how she survived knowing this may just be the conclusion of round one. The best way to describe her mental state during the week was analogous to a swan peacefully gliding across the water, while underneath the surface the webbed feet were scurrying a mile a minute.

Monday morning the telephone rang just as she was walking out of the door. Spinning around to hopefully grab the receiver before the caller hung up, she tripped over the cord and went sprawling across the floor. For some reason the caller was persistent, for it took Ellen a moment or two to collect herself and finally answer the phone. It was Charles checking to see how she was doing. Oh... could she give him a whopper of a story as she sat on the floor with her right knee starting to swell. If this was how the week was going to start out, she then contemplated calling in sick and returning to bed. No, she thought I can't do that, so out the door she hobbled, arriving at work exactly at nine o'clock.

On her desk was a notice from the manager informing Ellen that a few of her staff were displeased with her leadership and it was imperative they meet and talk. Sitting in his office, she wondered what shenanigans he was up to this time. If there was one thing she knew for sure, it was the strong team she had put together, not counting two employees that were hired before she came aboard. And if it wasn't the two employees that came strutting into the manager's office. It was well known throughout the company that Kevin was disappointed when he was not offered Ellen's job. Over the last two years Ellen tried to get him to buy-in and become a team player, and at one point actually thought she was successful. The young, blonde haired girl next to him was well known for dating everyone in the office. Her reputation preceeded her as to how she conducted business, mainly on her back.

The manager started the meeting by presenting a list of grievances. As soon as he started reading the complaints, Ellen knew they were concocted. The first complaint was that Ellen did not return telephone calls as fast as she should. However, the next complaint had a subtle underlying meaning. It seems Ellen expected the two employees present, to actually work. Her predecessor sloughed everything off and her end of the month numbers showed it. That is why the predecessor was no longer in the position, and that is why Ellen took her place.

Ellen said she had to hold back her laughter, for the folly was ridiculous. She knew that was the tip of the ice burg, the incidents to follow would start to escalate, and they did. After awhile the humor Ellen saw in the grievance list started to wane.

The day finally came when she called Charles and informed him that she was tired and dragged out from the constant pettiness that teetered on the border of harassment. Charles once again advised her to stick it out; everything was going to come to a head very soon. The next day he called to inform Ellen that the company showed an interest to mediate. Charles asked Ellen if she understood what mediation was all about. Replying "no" he immediately started to describe the ramifications involved.

Charlesstarted by reminding Ellen that mediation is offered as an alternative to what could possibly be a long drawn-out investigative case. Participation in the program is strictly confidential, voluntary, and requires consent from both the charging party and employer. If the mediation program fails, the charge will be returned to the EEOC for further investigation.

At first, the thought made the hair stand up on the back of Ellen's neck. Before consenting to mediation, she wanted to know exactly what was going to happen. Charles commented, "Ellen you sure are a tough cookie to work with, but I like it." If Charles only knew that underneath, she was shaking like a leaf. Ellen said she was surprised that Charles did not hear her knees knocking together.

In mediation, both parties meet at a legal office that specializes in the process. The attending attorney will sit at the head of a conference table. Ellen, you an I will sit on one side of the table with the company's representative on the other side. If they elect to use counsel, their attorney will be seated with them. The mediator will start by introducing everyone. He or she will then explain the goals and the rules of the mediation and encourage each side to work cooperatively in moving toward a settlement. Each party will then be invited to explain in his/her own words, exactly what the dispute involves. At this time, each party may offer some general ideas as how to resolve the case. While one party is presenting, the other party must not interrupt. Charles paused, intently looking at Ellen said: "I know you told me that your emotions are running high and you don't know if you can talk about the case with an open mind. Ellen, as your attorney, I will be more than willing to present the brief synopsis of the charge and will back it with a few pertinent points that justify the reason for our being there. Ellen feeling relieved thanked Charles for his caring and understanding.

"OK" Charles said, "let's continue." The mediator may encourage the parties to comment directly about what was stated in the opening statements. This is the time to determine the issues and how they should be addressed. The other side will have their chance to present any points they feel will have a bearing on the case. Sometimes this is used as a scare tactic, but don't let it get to you for the message they attempting to convey is; they will play hardball. In other words, what they want is for you to buckle so they can close their brief cases and go home early. Most likely, the opposing side will try to come up with some evidence that makes us think they are ready for a fight. "Ellen this is not the time to panic. Remember you are in the contoller's seat. "

Charles continued to explain that after everyone is finished, they would adjourn with the mediator to a private conference room in order to discuss a possible financial settlement. "The only true uncomfortable time is when everyone is in the conference room. Remember, you do not have to talk to anyone except your attorney. As a matter of fact you don't even have to look in the opposing side's direction…just pretend they are not there."

When we are all seated in a private conference room, the mediator will ask a few questions as to the relevance of the case. He will then proceed to ask how much it would take to settle. The mediator will then leave our conference room and go to the opposing sides room to discuss a possible settlement. His job, in essence is to travel back and forth from one room to the other, in hopes of seeking a remedy.

"Ellen are you ready to enter into mediation with the opposing side? Remember, if you are not completely pleased with the financial offer, you do not have to accept. We can proceed to arbitration or elect to take the case to a jury of your peers." Ellen thought for a moment and then in her straight forward manner, informed Charles that she was willing to enter into mediation.

Two weeks later the medaiton session was arranged. Everything went according to what Charles had described. There were no surprises for Ellen. The process appeared to be low keyed and rather stress free until the mediator presented the opposing side's settlement. Charles had warned Ellen the first settlement offer would be low, for the opposing side was starting the negotiating game by vying for a position. Charles did admit that even though he knew the offer would be low, he was shocked as to how low the opposing side came back with in the initial stages of the game.

When the mediator left, Charles turned toward Ellen and reminded her that she did not have to agree to a settlement at this time. However, it would be nice not to have to continue with the case but sit back and wait for the settlement check to arrive in the mail.

The first thing the mediator did when he entered the opposing side's room was to remind them as to the consequences of a jury trial. The opposing legal counsel agreed with the mediator, Ellen would prove to be a very believable defendant. Juries seemed to side with the little person and relish in doing in the corporate big shots. The opposition knew they had skeletons in the closet that needed to remain there, uncovering certain information would result in a messy court case.

Once again the mediator returned to the room and announced another extremely low settlement. The redness started in Ellen's neck and continued up into her face where she looked like Mount Vesuvius ready to explode. Jonah was right; she did have her pride to uphold and was not afraid to fight for it. Ellen commented sheepishly that she surprised herself when she blurted out: "Hell no, I am not going to be bought out for a mere measly five thousand dollars after what they did to me. Tell them I will see them in court and let a jury decide as to who is right." Charles sat back and casually smiled at the mediator. He looked like a wise old sage just dying to say "I told you so…she is not going to give up without a fight."

Well, to make a long story short that is not what happened. The opposing side after considering all ramifications involved conveniently came up with a third financial settlement. It was not the greatest, but it would substantiate her bluff of going to court. Although Charles had confidence in her and told her upfront that if she wanted to run with the case, he would more than happy to go along for the ride. Ellen thought Charles must have smoked his quota of dope back in the sixties. However, she did not mind, for at times she found him rather amusing. He made her laugh at times when she was about to break down and cry.

After leaving the mediation, Charles made a comment that greatly upset Ellen. As they were walking down the street, Charles casually stated that in the negotiations, the representative from the opposing side made a statement as how everyone at the company disliked Ellen. Immediately Ellen said to herself, what a petty, low life statement. With incredible composure Ellen stopped Charles in his tracks and said: "If I take the telephone list of all employees at the office, I could come up with seventy names of co-workers that would stick up for me in a deposition…and another forty percent that would have the guts to appear on my behalf in court. What side are you on Charles?" Ellen turned angrily and abruptly walked away. As soon as she entered her apartment, she found herself telephoning Jonah and sharing the day's events.

The first thing out of Jonah's mouth was "Hey, I think you did one heck of a job in the mediation." He proudly commented that he was impressed with her fortitude and tenacity. Jonah stated hat he was pleased with her for not allowing herself be railroaded as many have been in the past. Jonah continued to say, "Many people in your situation would have backed down, put their tails through their legs and high tailed it out of there." Nevertheless, he was impressed that Ellen stood her ground and would not be shaken. He always knew she had guts, and really was not surprised when it came out in the mediation.

Interestingly, Jonah appeared to be enjoying the dramatics of Ellen's situation. He seemed to relish in the idea that he may have the chance to be of assistance. Thinking back after the divorce, all Ellen wanted was for Jonah to ride off into the sunset and never be heard of again. Nevertheless, here he was sitting in front of her when she desperately needed someone.

Throughout the marriage Jonah was never there. It took the divorce and this situation to show Ellen that he really did love her. Sometimes life works in mysterious ways.

Action: It was interesting according to Ellen that the same humiliating way management treated her in the workplace was the same way they were trying to treat her in mediation. This completely infuriated her and helped make the decision easier in that she would take the case to court. This company was going to be taught a lesson, and that is you can't treat qualified employees with disrespect and get away with it. Charles realizing what was going on quickly interceded and reminded Ellen that a court is not a place for revenge. He felt part of his job was representing her and the other part was to explain the parmaters of the legal system.

The opposing side in this case, during the mediation process, arrived at the realization that Ellen was not going to give up without a legal fight. After due consideration, the opposing side felt it was better to end the dispute with a financial settlement. Charles reiterated that it would be best to take the money and end the case. He once again reminded Ellen of the long, arduous process of continuing into court. And then stated that even though they had a strong case, things can always go wrong to where the verdict may not be in Ellen's favor. Charles suggested that he felt it was best for Ellen to accept the settlement and get on with her life. And she did.

Recourse: The law states, employer have full rights to set or change company standards and policies. Although when a long-term employee (such as Ellen) who has received excellent reviews, must be considered for a promotion. She cannot simply be passed over lightly.

The manager also committed a mistake when he told Ellen that part of the reason for not getting the promotion was because of her age. Ellen being in a protected group had the strong arm of the law behind her.

19

THE EQUAL EMPLOYMENT OPPORTUNITY COMMISSION

The United States *Equal Employment Opportunity Commission (EEOC)*

Several of the women interviewed in the study were familiar with the *Equal Employment Opportunity Commission.* A few openly admitted they knew of the Commission but became frightened at the mere thought of becoming involved in a nasty, long drawn and expensive legal fight.

The *EEOC* is setup to protect the rights of an individual that experience(s) some type of discrimination or harassment in the workplace.

What is discrimination? The act or acts of treating individuals differently from others, especially because of some characteristic or membership, such as race, sex, religion or national origin.

What is harassment? Any annoying or offensive conduct in the workplace directed toward an employee or a group of employees based on color, race, religion, sex, disability, national origin, or age.

Discrimination affects individuals if:

- The individual is over forty years of age.
- The individual is African American, Hispanic, Asian or Native American (or a member of another minority group)
- The individual's family are natives of different countries in the world (non-American)
- The individual is Christian, Buddhist, Catholic, Hindu, Protestant, etc.
- The individual has a bad back, is wheel chair bound, wears prosthesis, or has a communicable disease.

If you qualify for any of the above, then you are classified as a member of a protected group. For some reason you do not qualify for any of the above reason(s), then *reverse discrimination* can be used. *Reverse Discrimination* means that just because the person does not qualify for a protected group that he/she can be discriminated against. No matter what side of the fence you fall on, employers are restricted from discrimination against you in the workplace. (protected group member, or not)

The following are simplified definitions of types of discrimination:

- **Race**: This type of discrimination occurs when an employer treats an employee differently due to the employee's race or characteristics that is related to the employer's race.

- **Sex**: This type of discrimination occurs when an employer treats an employee differently due to the employee's sex or because of a characteristic that is related to the employee's sex.

- **National Origin**: This type of discrimination occurs when an employer treats an employee differently due to the country the employee came from or because of the employee's ancestry.

- **Religion**: This type of discrimination occurs when an employer treats an employee differently due to the employee's religious beliefs or lack of religious beliefs. Under certain circumstances, the employer may be required to provide a reasonable accommodation which must not cause an undue hardship for the employer.

- **Age**: This type of discrimination refers to individuals over the age of forty that are treated unfairly in the workplace. This type of discrimination only applies to employers who have at least 20 employees.

- **Disability**: This type of discrimination occurs when an employer treats an employee differently due to the employee's disability, or perceived by the employer as being disabled.

- **Equal Pay Act**: This act protects women and men who perform equal work in the same establishment.

An employer is legally accountable for:

1. Harassment based on color, race, religion, sex, disability, national origin, or age.
2. Hiring and Firing legalities (policies)
3. Testing (drug competency, etc.)
4. Use of company facilities
5. Compensation, assignment or classification of employees
6. Recruitment
7. Transfer, promotion, layoff, or recall
8. Training and apprenticeship programs
9. Job advertisements
10. Fringe benefits
11. Conditions and terms of employment
12. Pay, retirement plans, and disability leave

The following statistics prove that you are not alone when it comes to being discriminated or harassed in the workplace. Unfortunately, the statistics only illustrate the number of individuals that were able (possibly because of financial means) to take action.

Statistics: In 1998 The U.S. Equal Employment Opportunity Commission reported the following employment charges:

Total Employees to file a claim:	41,886,106
Female:	19,696,182 (47.0%)
Male:	22,187,924 (53.0%)

Females & Males combined: (no gender breakdown available)

Age	15,191 (19.1%)
Disability	17,806 (22.4%)
Equal Pay Act	1,071 (1.3%)
National Origin	6,778 (8.5%)
Religion	1,786 (2.2%)
Sex	24,454 (30.7%)

RIGHTS: Remember that if you have been violated in some, shape or form in the workplace, do not be apprehensive and reluctant to defend yourself. Anyone who believes that her employment rights have been violated may file a charge of discrimination with the EEOC. Remember that before going through all the trouble to file a claim with the EEOC, the agency only accepts claims against employers that have 15 or more employees.

INFORMATION ON FILING A CLAIM: This claim may be filed, mailed or presented in person at the closest EEOC office. You can obtain the telephone number by checking your local telephone directory or call 1-800-669-4000 (voice) or 1-800-669-6820 to contact the nearest EEOC office for specific information on the procedures of filing a charge.

There are two courses of action to pursue at the EEOC.

File a claim:

1. Request the agency to conduct its own investigation and make a finding.

2. Request for a *"Right to Sue" authorization letter*Explanation of letter: In order to advance directly to the US District Court to file a *lawsuit* for *damages* an individual must request a *"Right to Sue" letter*. When the authorization let-

ter is formally requested, the EEOC will close its file and issue the *"Right to Sue" letter*...typically within 7-10 days. Remember, that before an individual can sue their employer in US District Court for *discrimination* or *harassment,* the above requirements must be met.

The *EEOC* uses the following forms:

1. Checklist Data Information Required to Process a *Right to Sue* (2 pages)

2. Fill in the Blank form letter to request a *"Right to Sue"* authorization. Different local offices may have additional required forms. It is best to telephone the office and ask for exact information.

REQUIRED INFORMATION: Be aware that the forms are signed under the penalty of perjury. Separate claim forms should be filed for each employee against whom a claim is being made, and for the company. The employee is required to submit the following information in order to file a *charge*:

-   Complaining person's name, address, and telephone number.

-   Name, address, and telephone number of the employer or agency that is alleged to have caused the discrimination.

-   Short description of the event(s) that caused the complaining person to believe that her rights were violated.

-   Dates of the alleged violation(s).

Example:
Jane Downing
4433 Ash St.,
Joplin, MO 44556
777-666-8989

Stewart Manufacturing
1234 Main St,
Joplin, MO 44556

Description: I was passed over for a promotion and was informed it was because I am over forty years old. I had the strongest qualifications and most extensive qualifications of any of the prospects. The job went to a male, age twenty-two, and with no experience.

Date: 4-12-2000

TIMING: Time is of the essence when filing a claim with the EEOC. All areas enforced by the EEOC, except the *Equal Pay Act*, require filing a charge within a specific time. The following are the rules to be adhered to:

• In order to protect your rights, a charge must be filed with the *EEOC* within 180 days from the date of the alleged violation.

• The above time regulations do not apply to claims under the *Equal Pay Act (EPA)*. This is because under this specific Act individuals are not required to file a charge with the *EEOC* first in order to have the right to sue in court. Keep in mind that since many *EPA* claims also raise (Title VII) *sex discrimination* issues, it may be advisable to file *charges* under both laws within the time limits indicated. The individual's legal counsel responsibility is to take care of the time issue involved.

• When discrimination is suspected it is advisable to contact the *EEOC* immediately. The individual's lawyer will take care of contacting the *EEOC*.
  Note: Time requirements may vary from state to state. Check with the *EEOC* office in the state where you reside.

  ATER THE CHARGE IS FILED: The employer is notified that a charge has been filed. If the initial facts appear to support a legal violation, a charge may be assigned for priority investigation. When the evidence in the case is not as strong, the charge may require a follow-up investigation in order to determine whether a violation has occurred.

EEOC PROCEDURES:

- The EEOC is willing to work with the parties involved in the case and will seek to settle a charge at any stage if both parties mutually agree. If for some reason(s) settlement efforts are not achieved then the investigation continues.

- When investigating a charge, the EEOC may require the following:

  1. Written requests for information

  2. Interview people

  3. Review documents

  4. If needed, visit the facility where the alleged violation occurred

When the investigation is complete, the *EEOC* will discuss the evidence with the charging party or the employer.

DISMISSED CHARGE:

- If the *EEOC* does not feel that further investigation will establish grounds for a violation of law.

- May be dismissed at the time it is filed

- May be dismissed at any time if an initial in-depth interview does not produce evidence to support the claim

Mediation: *Mediation* is a program that is offered as an alternative action to a lengthy time consuming claim. This is an informal process in which a neutral-third party assists both sides in reaching a voluntary resolution. The decision to mediate is completely voluntary for both sides.

It has been reported by Jose, Welch, and McDermott (2000) the majority of employers and charging parties that have participated in mediation programs are highly pleased with the program. The EEOC sites the results as a product of efficiency and fairness for both employers and charging parties. The resolution of disputes in less than 100 days marks the success of the program.

Advantages of Mediation:

• Efficient fair process

• Saves time and money

• Most conflicts are resolved in one session (consisting of 1-5 hours)

• Strictly confidential

• Settlements reached during mediation do not constitute an admission of guilt by the employer in reference to violation(s) of EEOC enforced laws

• Avoids unnecessary and lengthy litigation

NOTE: For additional information concerning the EEOC Mediation Program, see the web page: **http://www.eeoc.gov/**

Mediator: The responsibility of the mediator is to assist both parties explore, examine, and hopefully reconcile differences. Only professionals that are experienced and trained in mediation and equal employment opportunity law are assigned to partake in charges filed with the EEOC. These individuals are neutral, unbiased third parties that have no stake in the outcome of the case. Remember, that the EEOC does not require parties involved to agree to mediation. If a resolution is not achieved in the mediation session then the EEOC will continue investigating the charge.

Mediation appears like a good, sensible, and non-threatening way to proceed. However, if the opposing side is not willing to negotiate then mediation cannot take place. In some cases if the claim has gone on for a considerable length of time, nothing anyone can say will help. The other side will naturally oppose anything suggested.

Sometimes the best way to coax a belligerent party to cooperate and mediate is to go through an indirect, third party. In essence what this means is that the individual has to locate a mediation organization appropriate for the specific dispute. Organizations are generally better skilled at convincing angry parties to mediate. In the case of a personal (neighborhood) dispute, local community mediation boards are available. For business divorce disputes, an individual can locate an organization in the telephone yellow pages under mediation.

After locating several organizations:

1. Telephone the organization and explain the situation.

2. Select the appropriate organization for the case.

3. Write a short but polite letter to the disputing party explaining the mediation. Include in the letter that a mediation service will be contacted.
    NOTE: If the individual has retained counsel, the above will be taken care of by the legal office of the attorney, or just by the attorney.

4. Once the mediation service has been notified, a letter will be sent by the service to the disputing party explaining mediation and its benefits.

5. If there is no response within a week or two, a case manager will be assigned the case.

6. If the opposing side refuses to mediate on the advice of their attorney, then the case manager will contact their attorney and discuss the case. This is an attempt to get both sides to mediate.

If the opposing party refuses to mediate, or if there is no satisfaction derived out of the mediation then there are other ways to proceed. What ever way is decided upon, it has to be better than filing a lawsuit and ending up in court. Remember, that lawsuits can prove to be incredibly expensive, time consuming, and emotionally draining.

Nevertheless, if for some reason one party refused mediation, try suggesting arbitration. This is another out of court process of dispute reconciliation. Arbitration requires the parties involved to have the dispute(s) decided by an arbitrator and not in a court of law.

An arbitrator is a type of private judge. The arbitration hearing is much less formal than a court hearing. There is usually no right to appeal an arbitrator's ruling, so when the judgment is made, it is final. As to the expense of arbitration, sometimes it can be rather inexpensive and other times, depending on the subject matter, may prove to be extremely expensive. In employment disputes, it is not often likely for an individual to go into arbitration after mediation. In other type of cases, arbitration is quite common. Even though there are these other processes for conflict resolution than going to court, if one party refuses mediation, try suggesting arbitration.

Timing: The mediation process usually is planned to take place in the early stages of the claim (if agreed upon by both parties). Both sides are contacted to establish or set an agreed upon time.

The EEOC saves a substantial expense by avoiding the investigation of the charge. Mediation softens the process of filing a discrimination charge by informally attempting to resolve the conflict(s). When charges are seen to be drawn out over a lengthy time period, sides usually harden their positions and resolutions are then more difficult to accomplish. Both sides will be contacted as to an agreed upon time.

The process is deemed to be efficient, time saving, and less costly than other legal avenues of resolution. The majority of mediations are completed in one session, which typically lasts from one to five or six hours.

Location: Both sides will be contacted to set a mutually convenient place.

Required attendance: The charging party and the employer or a designated representative should attend the mediation session. If a person is going to represent the employer then he or she should be familiar with the facts of the case and have the authority to settle the charge on behalf of the employer.

Legal Council involvement: Although it is not necessary to have an attorney in order to participate in the mediation program, it lessens the degree of stress and apprehension. Either side may elect to have an attorney represent with them. The mediator's job is to decide what role the attorney(s) will play during the program. In most instances, the mediator will ask legal counsel(s) to provide appropriate advice. If a party or parties plan to bring professional assistance to the mediation, it would be beneficial to contact the mediator prior to the session.

Confidentiality: The EEOC adheres to strict confidentiality in concern with its mediation program. Everyone involved must sign agreements that all evidence presented during the mediation process be kept private. To ensure confidentiality these procedures are followed:

- No transcriptions or tape recording allowed

- Notes taken during mediation are destroyed

- Records/documents provided by either side during the mediation are destroyed

- Mediation is kept separate from all EEOC's investigative and litigation functions

If the parties cannot arrive at an amiable settlement agreement then the options afforded consist of proceeding to arbitration or court.

Arbitration is another step in the legal forum that an individual may elect in attempting to reconcile the dispute. Arbitration requires the parties involved to have any dispute(s) decided by an arbitrator and not in court. An arbitrator is a type of private judge. The arbitration hearing is much less formal than a court hearing. There is usually no right to appeal an arbitrator's ruling, so when the judgment is made, it is final.

In employment disputes, it is not often likely for an individual to go into arbitration after mediation. In other type of cases, arbitration is common.

Cost: There is no required fee for mediation.

Eligible charges: The EEOC evaluates each charge to determine whether it is appropriate for the mediation program. Factors examined are: (1) the nature of the case, (2) the relationship of parties involved, (3) the complexity and size of the case, (4) and the type and amount of relief sought by the charging party. Charges that The EEOC classifies as being without merit are not eligible for mediation.

No resolution: If for some reason(s) the charge is not resolved during the mediation process, it is then returned to a specified investigative unit and handled like any other charge.

Subsequent use of information: Information revealed during the mediation session cannot be disclosed to anyone including other EEOC personnel. Remember that the entire process is strictly confidential; therefore, information disclosed cannot be used during any subsequent investigation.

Agreement compliance: An agreement resolving a charge of discrimination filed with the EEOC during a mediation process is enforceable in a court of law. If either party feels that the other party has failed to comply with a mediated settlement agreement, he or she should contact the EEOC immediately.

Mediation program information: Telephone: (800) 669-4000 or Internet: **http://www.eeoc.gov**

EEOC field offices in alphabetical order are listed in Chapter 18 'General but Useful Information'

Information required filing a complaint:

Read: The EEOC processes cases of discrimination and unfair practices based on race, color, national origin, sex, age, religion and disability. If you feel that you have been discriminated against or subjected to unfair practices, your request may fall within the authority of the Commission.

1. The following information must be provided: (typed or legible… please use ink)

    a. **WHO?** Provide a name(s) as to discriminated against you or subjected you to unfair practices.

    b. **WHEN?** Dates (include month and year)

    c. **WHERE:** The location where the discrimination or unfair practice took place.

    d. **WHAT?** Describe what happened.

2. All complaints are strictly confidential and will be assigned a number when filed. When referring to the complaint, use the assigned number.

3. When the complaint is received, it will be carefully reviewed. At that time, a team of Commission members will contact you to discuss specific details of the complaint.

4. If for some reason(s) the Commission has no jurisdiction to proceed, you will be contacted and referred to the appropriate agency for processing.

5. The complaint must be filed within 180 days from the date of the discrimination or unfair practice(s).

Standard information required:

1. Name

2. Address

3. Home telephone

4. Work telephone

5. Social Security number

6. Gender (male or female)

7. Date of birth

8. Alternate contact name and telephone number

9. Type of Employment

10. Action taken against you

    a. Wages

    b. Promotion

    c. Hiring

    d. Discharge

    e. Suspension

11. Date(s) of Discrimination:

12. Basis:

    a.   Race

    b.   Color

    c.   Age

    d.   Sex

    e.   National Origin/Ancestry

    f.   Religion

    g.   Disability

13. Marital Status

14. Retaliation

15. Who initiated the complaint?

16. What actions were taken?

17. How were you treated differently?

18. What do you wish to accomplish with this complaint?

19. List any documents, information, records that would be significant to your complaint

20. Item(s) location

21. List potential witness(s)

22. Name(s) and telephone number(s) of witness(s)

23. If the mediation program were appropriate for your case, would you consider it?

24. The above information requires a notary

*Internet: Equal Employment Opportunity Commission site, 6-2000.

*Clapp, J.E. (1996). Random House Webster's Legal Dictionary. New York. Random House.

*Lewin, J.G. (1996). Every Employee's Guide to the Law, New York. Pantheon Books

20

GENERAL BUT USEFUL INFORMATION

Legal Representation: It is not necessary to have an attorney in order to take part in a mediation program. Either or both sides may elect to have legal counsel. If an individual decides to hire a professional legal advisor, be sure the type of payment is agreed upon up front. Unfortunate surprises (especially a steep legal bill) are not what most individuals welcome.

If you have a case that involves property or legal rights, it may be in your best interest to at least consult with a lawyer in order to discuss the probability of a settlement. It may also be advisable to condition any agreement made based on a lawyer's approval.

When selecting legal counsel make sure your intentions are understood upfront. How do you want to use the attorney's services?

1. Lawyer coach you initially

2. Lawyer coach you on a continuous basis

3. Lawyer that understands and supports mediation

4. Lawyer available to review specific documents

Questions to ask the lawyer:

1. Have you worked with any clients going through mediation?

2. Have you been trained in mediation? (request specifics...)

Now comes the key question..."how do I find a good lawyer?"

1. Do not select a name out of the yellow pages

2. Do not answer an advertisement in the local paper

But:

1. Talk to friends…they may know someone who had a similar case

2. Network at church, the fitness club, etc.

Then: set up an interview with the prospective lawyer…most lawyers will meet with an individual for at least a half hour with no fee charged.

Legal Fees/Costs: A client a responsibility financially:

1. Pay the attorney's fees for services rendered in reference to the case

2. Court costs and litigation costs (this applies only if the case goes to court)

There are creative ways to negotiate the fees. The most important thing to remember is agree upfront, before any work is completed, as to the type of payment(s). Speaking from experience it is best to use the caveman style of getting all terms etched in stone. A person does not have to go to that extreme, but take note, get things in writing! It will keep from problems erupting down the road.

Most attorneys' will sit down and discuss different types of payment. Here are a few options:

1. Contingency Fee Arrangement: Most attorneys will agree to handle cases on a contingency fee basis. This is where the legal fees are paid by the client (you) only when the case is settled. An arbitration award, judgment or other type of resolution that entails a monetary exchange generates fees. What is great about this type of fee payment is, if there is no recovery (money awarded) for the client, then there are no attorney's fees.

2. Hourly Fee Arrangement: In some special situations and hourly rate may be charged. For instance, if you only need counseling,

forms completed and delivered…then it may be the right way to go. Ask immediately what the attorney's rate is, for you do not want to have sticker shock when you get his/her bill. Attorney's fees are steep, ranging from $120.00 per hour to $400.00. (note: this is a generalized range)

3. Contingency and Hourly Arrangement: Depending on the situation, this plan may work for you. A client will agree upon a payment upfront and then at the time of execution of the Retainer Agreement, the attorney will take an agreed upon percentage.

Costs: Most costs consist of products/services obtained by third parties in connection with the litigation and court expenses. The following is a list of some typical costs an individual may incur:

1. Expert witness fees

2. Court reporting

3. Court filing fees

4. Postage

5. Fax transmissions

6. Photocopying

7. Process service fees

When discussing payments with the attorney, ask if there are any add-on charges. You do not need any unwanted surprise.

How to Save on Legal Fees: Lawyers are expensive, but there are ways to control legal fees. Here are a few suggestions:

1. Request your lawyer to be your advisor, similar to a coach/athlete relationship. If you are able physically and emotionally, try to do

all the research yourself. The Internet can be your best place for resources, and most of the time it is free. Helping yourself by doing a lot of the preliminary work may possibly save 10% to 20% of what it would cost to hire a lawyer to perform the entire job. Many of the lawyers commented that most of their clients dropped all responsibility as soon as they entered the legal offices. Discuss upfront as to how you would like the lawyer to assist you in your case.

2. The use of non-lawyer type professionals is becoming more popular. Many of these individuals are able to perform the same tasks as the lawyers, while charging a significantly lower rate. A combination of the above skills is quite desirable.

    a. Initial meeting with the lawyer to find out what research and documents are needed.

    b. Contact a non-lawyer and explain the requirements. Most of these people work on an hourly basis. Establish what the time commitment may be and what the hourly rate is. Sometimes a flat rate may be agreed upon ahead of time.

    c. Send the documents to the lawyer for his/her review

    d. Arrange a meeting to discuss actions to pursue

3. If you have a variety of issues to address, then organize and prioritize the list. Simple organization will save you a lot of money.

4. Paying your bills on time. This will establish a valued relationship between client and lawyer. If for some reason you cannot pay the bill on time, telephone and explain the reason(s) and what action you are planning to take.

Court: Try to mediate your case, maybe select arbitration, but the last place you want to go and that is to court. Mediation (as previously discussed) is informal, everyone speaks English and not legalize, procedures are kept to a minimum, and a decision is not made unless you agree. Arbitration has a few more strict rules. When you go into arbitration, a third party makes a final judgment, one that you not only have to accept, but live with. If all fails and you have no choice, then go to court.

Preparation for a court case is not always complicated, but time consuming, stressful, and can be (in certain circumstances) expensive. If all possible, retain legal counsel. Experiencing a court case will feel like you are on the world's largest roller coaster. There is a required protocol in court. This is especially true if your case is brought before a judge without a jury. Here are a few suggestions:

1. Attend a few trials involving similar situations as to your case. What you will normally see is:

    a. Opening statement: Each party presents an overview of his/her case that includes what they expect to prove.

    b. Direct examination: This is the time the plaintiff presents his/her testimony as to what happened. This is supported by witness's statements and other pertinent evidence.

2. Cross-examination: After each of the plaintiff's witnesses testifies, the defendant has the opportunity to conduct a cross-examination. The defendant attempts to prove the witnesses false and non-credible and his or her version true.

3. Closing Argument: Each side is allowed to explain to the judge or jury as to why they should win.

4. Each side gets to present a closing argument during which time tries to explain

It is strongly suggested that the reader should study books especially written on the subject of how to act and what to expect in court. The majority of these books will address some of the following:

5. Address the judge as "your honor" and not Judge Hokum or Jones.

6. Do not get up and repeat everything you once said.

7. Do not interrupt the opposing side, wait for your turn.

It would be helpful to keep a trial notebook that outlines all the nuances of your trial. Think of this step as keeping a diary. Note everything that happens, for you may need it some point in time. Use this as a reference, and a recall mechanism.

Start your notebook by outlining your goals. Next, organize a series of questions you feel pertinent to the case that you can either address the plaintiff, the plaintiff's witnesses, or both. Also, have a list of critical questions to be used in your cross-examination. The notebook may be reviewed with your legal counsel to make sure everyone is in accord, in other words no conflicting views.

If you are representing yourself, and the opposing side's lawyer starts pontificating by using legal reference numbers, ask the judge permission to stop him or her. Explain to the judge that you are representing yourself due to a lack of finances and you would appreciate it if the judge could apply the right law. Since you do not have a law background, you are relying on his or her expertise and professionalism.

Appropriate Channels to Seek Help...Federal and State Contact Numbers:

AREA	TITLE	AGENCY	CONTACT NUMBER
American with Disabilities Act	Information line and home page	Federal	800-514-0301
COBRA: Portability of Insurance Law	Continuation of Insurance coverage	Federal	206-553-4244

ERISA: Pension, Welfare Benefits	Pensions plans, retirement, and Employee profit Sharing	Federal	202-219-8776
Dept. of Labor	Wage and hour	Federal	503-326-3057
Technical questions	minimum wage		503-326-3057
Minimum wage			
Employment Department	Affirmative action, alien labor certification,	State	800-237-3710
Equal	Information center	Federal	800-6693362
Employment Opportunity Commission	EEOC		http://www.eeoc.gov
Information	Federal agency Information	Federal	800-688-9889
Information	State agency Information	State	503-378-6500
Internal Revenue Service	Federal taxes & withholding	Federal	800-829-1040
			http://www.irs.ustreas.gov
Legal Research	Web sites for	Private	http://www.FindLaw.com

| Preferred Worker Program, Workers' Compensation | Return of injured workers | State | 503-947-7568 |

Equal Employment Opportunity Commission (EEOC) Field Offices

Mediation Contact List:

City	Telephone #
Albuquerque	(505) 248-5193
Atlanta	(404) 562-6841
Baltimore	(410) 962-6606
Birmingham	(205) 731-0175
Charlotte	(704) 344-6684
Chicago	(312) 353-2421
Cleveland	(216) 522-8441
Dallas	(214) 665-3363
Denver	(303) 866-1950
Houston	(713) 209-3439
Indianapolis	(317) 226-5162
Los Angeles	(213) 894-1121
Memphis	(901) 544-0112
Miami	(305) 536-5721
Milwaukee	(414) 297-1115
New York	(212) 748-8399
Philadelphia	(215) 451-5505
Phoenix	(602) 640-5072
San Antonio	(210) 281-7600
San Francisco	(415) 356-5044

Seattle	(206) 220-6882
St. Louis	(913) 551-5802
Washington D.C.	(202) 632-1115

21

LEGAL TERMS DEFINED

Legal Definitions: (italicized legal terms in the text defined)

A

Administrative employee: An employee who is exempt from federal laws requiring overtime pay because the individual earns at least $250 per week. This person' responsibilities include performing sophisticated work involving the company's policies or business operations, in which discretion and judgment are used.

Adverse impact: When the effect of a company policy or work rule (even when the rule appears to be impartial) falls heavily on individuals in a protected group of workers than on other workers.

Agency: A relationship between two people, or entities, whereby one is authorized to act on behalf or range of matters of another.

Age Discrimination (ADEA): The federal law that prohibits discrimination in the workplace against employees over the age of 40. Note, this only applies to employers who have at least 20 employees.

Americans With Disabilities Act (ADA): A federal law that prohibits discrimination against individuals with physical or mental disabilities in employment, public services and places of public accommodation.

Arbitration: A stated provision in a contract that requires the parties involved to have any dispute(s) decided by an arbitrator and not in court. An arbitrator is a type of private judge. The arbitration hearing is much less formal than a court hearing. There is usually no right to appeal an arbitrator's ruling.

At-will employment: An employment relationship in which either the employee or the employer may terminate the employment at any time for any reason.

B

Bench Trial: A trial before a judge without a jury.

Benefits: The term "benefits" refer to health, dental, vision, life, and disability insurance. Quite often with insurance premiums, the employer pays a part or sometimes the entirety. Benefits also include pension and retirement.

Burden of Proof: A party's responsibility of convincing the decision-maker in a trial that the party's version of the facts is true

C

Case: A term that usually refers to a lawsuit.

Charge: A formal allegation that a person has violated a specific criminal law.

Claim: An assertion that an individual is entitled to something. In the federal courts and throughout many states an assertion of facts that if true, would legally entitle the claimant to judgment in a civil case.

COBRA: This is an abbreviation of the "Consolidated Omnibus Budget Reconciliation Act. It is the federal law that requires certain employers to continue to provide health benefits to employees for a limited-specified time after the employee' termination.

Compensation: The salary paid by an employer to an employee for work performed in the job. Compensation is paid as either a salary or an hourly rate.

Complaint: Papers filed with a court clerk by the plaintiff to initiate a lawsuit by spelling out the facts and the legal claims.

Concurrent: This refers to lawsuits that the EEOC files against an employer alleging a claim of employment discrimination.

Constructive discharge: An act or acts by the employer that makes the job unbearable. The employee resigns and is still permitted to file a lawsuit or collect unemployment.

Contract: The broad definition is any legally enforceable promise.

Contingency fee: A method of paying an attorney for legal representation by which, instead if an hourly or per job fee, the legal counsel receives a percentage of the money the client obtains after settling or winning the case.

Court Costs: The fees charged for the use of the court. These costs include: an initial filing fee, depositions, summon serving, complaint and other court papers, court reporter, jurors stipend, photocopy court papers/exhibits. Court costs are paid by both parties as the case progresses, but ultimately, the losing party will be responsible for both parties costs.

D

Damages: In a lawsuit this is money awarded to one party base on injury or loss caused by the other. The following are different types of damages: (1) general damages are intended to cover injuries for which an exact dollar amount cannot be calculated, (2) compensatory damage cover actual injury or economic loss, (3) nominal damages are used when a jury finds favor of one party to a lawsuit, (4) punitive damages are awarded over and above special and general damages to punish a losing party's willful or malicious misconduct, (5) special damages cover the winning party's out-of-pocket-costs, (6) statutory damages are the authority given to a judge to pay damages, and (7) treble damages are triple the amount plus the amount it lost as a result of the other party's illegal conduct.

Defendant: The individual against whom a lawsuit is filed. Sometimes called the respondent.

Default judgment: A judgment obtained by an individual who files a lawsuit against an employer who failed to file papers defending the lawsuit.

Defamation: This is when someone lies about the individual to another person. Printed lies are classified as "libel" and spoken lies are called "slander."

Deposition: Tool used in pre-trial discovery. This is where one party questions the other party or witness(s) in the case. A deposition requires that all questions be answered under oath and recorded by a court reporter. This usually takes place in an attorney's office.

Direct suits: Lawsuits that the EEOC files against an employer alleging a claim of employment discrimination.

Discrimination: This occurs when an employer treats some workers differently from other workers. Not all discrimination is classified as illegal. Discrimination is illegal if it happens because the employee is in a certain protected class of people, for example: racial or religious minority.

Disability discrimination: This type of discrimination occurs when an employer treats an employee differently due to the employee has a disability, or perceived by the employer as disabled.

Discovery: The process of obtaining information in the possession of the opposing party.
This takes place after a lawsuit is filed. Discovery devices include: written interrogatories, depositions, requests for admission, and a request for document(s).

Disparate Treatment: This type of action occurs when an individual is treated differently from their peers.

E

Employee: An individual performs work for another person or company.

Employee Rights: At-will employees are protected from adverse action if the reason(s) for that specific action is an illegal reason. Reasons that prove illegal are based on federal law, which include: discrimination because of race, color, national origin, legal alienage, pregnancy, religion, age, disability and union activity. Several states have laws that protect employees on the same grounds as federal law. Some state and local laws protect employees against discrimination based on additional reason, such as marital status, sexual orientation or preference.

Employer: An individual or company who hires a person to perform work.

Equal Employment Opportunity Commission (EEOC): The federal agency responsible for handling complaints associated with discrimination in the workplace.
The organization was created by the Civil Rights Act of 1964 in order to administer and enforce prohibitions against workplace discrimination.

Equal Pay Act of 1963 (EPA) This act protects women and men who perform equal work in the same establishment .

Exempt employee: An individual who does not have the right to over-time pay.

Exit Interview: A dismissed, fired, or employee that resigns has the right to request an exit interview. The request is usually submitted to the employer's supervisor. At this time, the individual is allowed to express opinions as to the justification or lack of justification to the dismissal.

F

Fair Labor Standards Act: The federal law that governs employees wages, including payment of minimum wage and overtime.

G

Good ole boy system: Attitudes maintained by older male management. The thinking is "only males can perform a good job." Females should stay at home where they belong.

H

Harasser: This individual may be either a woman or a man. The title of the harasser may be: (1) supervisor, (2) agent of the employer, (3) supervisor in another department, or a (4) co-worker.

Harassment: This is a specific type of discrimination. It occurs when an employer or someone else in the workplace says or does something to make an employee feel uncomfortable or intimidated. Harassment proves to be illegal only if it is done because of the employee's sex, race, or other protected category classification.

Hostile Environment: Sexual harassment conduct that interferes with an individual's work performance or creates an intimidating, offensive workplace environment. This definition implicitly includes sexual advances, requests for sexual favors, and physical/verbal conduct that connotes a sexual nature.

I

Illegal: Discrimination in any form (either disparate or overt treatment) against a member of a protected class.

Implied employment contract: An employment contract between an employer and employee that is not written or verbal, but implied from the circumstances of the employee's position.

Institutional discrimination: This type of discrimination includes: different standards of review, less recognition of achievement, lower salary increases, denial of benefits or promotions, and denial of a fair grade.

Interrogatories: This requests the opposing party to answer certain questions in writing.

Intervention: This is where the EEOC joins a lawsuit that has been filed by a private plaintiff.

J

Judgment: A final court ruling resolving the principle questions in a lawsuit, and determining the obligations and rights of the opposing parties.

Judgment notwithstanding the verdict: At the end of a trial, a jury will render a verdict in favor of one of the parties. The losing party may then file a motion arguing that even if all the conflicts in the evidence are resolved, the verdict is still improper. If the judge agrees, the verdict will be set aside and a new judgment will be entered for the party initiating the motion.

Jury: A group of people selected to address and apply the law as stated by the ruling judge, to the facts of a case resulting in the rendering of a decision.

L

Lawsuit: If a settlement agreement cannot be reached and the agency has reasonable cause to believe the individual has a valid case, a right-to-sue notice will be issued. Once this notice is received, the individual has 90 days to file a lawsuit on the individual's behalf. Note: The individual can bring an age discrimination or Equal Pay Act lawsuit without receiving a right-to-sue-notice from the EEOC.

Liquidated damages: Equal to the amount of unpaid back wages. When liquidated damages in an action to recover wages are directly related to a FLSA violation, then payment is automatic. This refers to the individual who wins the case, will be awarded twice what the employer owes.

Litigation: The process of coordinating and pursuing a lawsuit.

M

Mediation: A less tense dispute resolution method designed to help assist parties resolve their own dispute(s) without going to court. In mediation, a neutral third party meets with the opposing side to aid them in finding a mutually satisfactory solution. The mediator does not have any power to impose a solution on the parties involved. This is an informal way to reach an agreement.

Misconduct: An individual violates an important workplace rule, for instance, stealing, sleeping on the job, or getting into a physical or verbal confrontation with another worker.

Motion for a new trial: After a jury or judge renders a verdict, the losing party may file a motion for a new trial based on the ground that their as some procedure mistake took place during the trial.

N

National origin discrimination: This type of discrimination occurs when an employer treats an employee differently due to the country the employee came from or because of the employee's ancestry.

Nepotism: Perceptions of favoritism in the workplace. This often occurs when relatives or spouses work together for the same employer.

O

Overt Discrimination: Direct actions taken that violates a person's space or damage to personal property. These acts are also classified as "hate crimes."

Overtime: Hours worked inn excess of 40 in a week. Overtime hours are usually paid at the rate of one and a half times an employee's regular pay rate.

P

Plaintiff: The person, corporation or other legal entity that initiates a lawsuit.

Professional employee: An employee who is exempt from laws requiring overtime pay. This is based on the high-level of training the employee has received. This person also has the authority to make important decisions without much supervision.

Prima facie: Used as a device to establish that if a certain set of facts are proven, then another fact is established prima facie. In some situations, the law may require prima facie case before proceeding to another step in the judicial process.

Punitive damages: Damages paid over and above compensation. If the plaintiff in a lawsuit proves that the defendant acted fraudulently or maliciously, the court may allow an award of this type. The concept behind this type of damages is for the court to punish the defendant and to set an example to other individuals that may be considering similar action.

Q

Quid Pro quo: Requests for sexual favors, unwelcome sexual advances, and other physical/verbal implications(s) promote this type of sexual harassment. Submission or rejection of sexual conduct by an individual is used as the basis for managerial-employment decisions directly or indirectly affecting the individual. Also included in this definition is such conduct made explicitly or implicitly as a condition of an individual's employment contract.

R

Racial discrimination: This type of discrimination occurs when an employer treats an employee differently due to the employee's race or characteristic that is related to the employee's race.

Reasonable accommodation: This is a change or modification to a job that makes it easier for an individual with a disability to perform the job.

Religious Discrimination: This type of discrimination occurs when an employer treats an employee differently due to the employee's religious beliefs. Under certain circumstances, the employer may be required to provide a reasonable accommodation (see definition listed above). This reasonable accommodation provided must not cause undue hardship for the employer.

Remedy: A legal action (almost always damages) that the law deems sufficient compensation.

Retaliation: An act or acts by an employer specifically directed to punish an employee for the employee's exercise of some right protected by the law.

Reverse: Appellate court nullifies the judgment of the lower court in a case on appeal due to some error in the court below. Sometimes a reversal disposes of the entire case; in other situations, it requires further proceedings.

Right to Sue Letter: The letter is issued by the EEOC. This letter gives the employee permission to file a discrimination lawsuit against his/her employer in a federal court.

S

Scapegoat: Individual setup in the workplace to take the blame for someone else's mistakes. Sometimes called the "fall person."

Severance package: Benefits (including money) offered by an employer to an employee to temporarily offset the employee's loss of a job.

Sex discrimination: This type of discrimination occurs when an employer treats an employee differently due to the employee's sex or because of a characteristic that is related to the employee's sex.

Sexual Harassments: This type of discrimination occurs when there is a hostile work environment. The form of harassment includes unwelcome sexual conduct related to the workplace.

Subpoena enforcement actions: These actions may be filed during the course of the investigation of a charge of discrimination where the respondent refuses to provide information relevant to the charge.

T

Termination: General term ending an individual's employment. Also is referred to as "discharge."

Title VII Civil Rights Act of 1964: Federal legislation designed to end discrimination based on religion, color, race or national origin. Title VI only applies to employers with 15 or more employees.

Torts: A wrongful act, other than a breach of contract, that results in injury to another person, property, reputation, or some other legally protected right or interest. The injured party is entitled to a remedy at law, usually in the form of damages.

U

Unwelcome Sexual Conduct: The individual regards the conduct as offensive or undesirable. The conduct is classified as sexually unwanted in reference to the individual not inciting or soliciting it.

V

Victim: The victim in a sexual harassment case may be either female or male. Please note that the victim does not have to be the individual harassed, but one that is affected by the offensive nature of the conduct.

W

Worker's compensation: The state system that requires an employer to pay an employee's benefits for injuries incurred on the job, no matter who is at fault for causing the injury(s).

Wrongful termination lawsuit: Lawsuit filed by an employee against a former employer who used illegal methods in terminating the employee. Also referred to as a "wrongful discharge lawsuit."

*Internet: Equal Employment Opportunity Commission site, 6-2000.
*Clapp, J.E. (1996). Random House Webster's Legal Dictionary. New York. Random House.
*Lewin, J.G. (1996). Every Employee's Guide to the Law, New York. Pantheon Books.

0-595-24377-0

www.ingramcontent.com/pod-product-compliance
Lightning Source LLC
Chambersburg PA
CBHW061355280526
45784CB00001B/269